This student workbook is intended to reinforce your understanding of the three units of substantive content (scientific explanations and evidence), plus the procedural content (How Science Works), on the single award GCSE Biology specification from AQA.

Every worksheet is cross-referenced to the revision and classroom companion *AQA GCSE Biology*, published by Letts and Lonsdale.

The questions in your objective tests / written exams will combine elements from both types of content, so to answer them you will have to recall relevant scientific facts and draw upon your knowledge of how science works.

The questions on pages 4–11 of this workbook will test your understanding of the key concepts covered in How Science Works. In addition, there are individual How Science Works question pages throughout this book, which are designed to make sure you know how to apply your knowledge, for example, to evaluate topical social-scientific issues.

HT In this workbook, any questions that cover content which will only be tested on Higher Tier test papers appear inside clearly labelled boxes.

A Note to Teachers

The pages in this workbook can be used as…
- classwork sheets – students can use the revision guide to answer the questions
- harder classwork sheets – pupils study the topic and then answer the questions without using the revision guide
- easy-to-mark homework sheets – to test pupils' understanding and reinforce their learning
- the basis for learning homework tasks which are then tested in subsequent lessons
- test material for topics or entire units
- a structured revision programme prior to the objective tests / written exams.

Answers to these worksheets are available to order.

ISBN: 978-1-905129-5

Published by Letts and Lonsdale.

Project editor: Rebecca Skinner

Cover and concept design: Sarah Duxbury

Design: Little Red Dog Design

© 2006, 2007, 2009 Letts and Lonsdale

All rights reserved. No part of this publication may be reproduced, stored in a retrieval system, or transmitted, in any form or by any means, electronic, mechanical, photocopying, recording or otherwise, without the prior permission of Letts and Lonsdale.

Letts and Lonsdale make every effort to ensure that all paper used in our books is made from wood pulp obtained from well-managed forests, controlled sources and recycled wood or fibre.

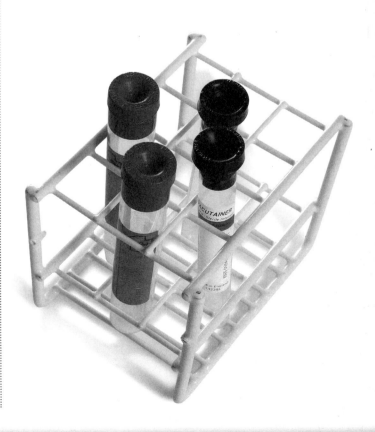

Contents

Contents

4 How Science Works (10.1–10.9)

Unit 1

12 How do human bodies respond to changes inside them and to their environment? (11.1)
17 What can we do to keep our bodies healthy? (11.2)
21 How do we use / abuse medical and recreational drugs? (11.3)
28 What causes infectious diseases and how can our bodies defend themselves against them? (11.4)
32 What determines where particular species live and how many of them there are? (11.5)
35 Why are individuals of the same species different from each other? What new methods do we have for producing plants and animals with the characteristics we prefer? (11.6)
39 Why have some species of plants and animals died out? How do new species of plants and animals develop? (11.7)
42 How do humans affect the environment? (11.8)
48 Key Words

Unit 2

49 What are animals and plants built from? (12.1)
51 How do dissolved substances get into and out of cells? (12.2)
52 How do plants obtain the food they need to live and grow? (12.3)
55 What happens to energy and biomass at each stage in a food chain? (12.4)
58 What happens to the waste material produced by plants and animals? (12.5)
59 What are enzymes and what are some of their functions? (12.6)
63 How do our bodies keep internal conditions constant? (12.7)
67 Which human characteristics show a simple pattern of inheritance? (12.8)
76 Key Words

Unit 3

78 How do dissolved materials get into and out of animals and plants? (13.1)
81 How are dissolved materials transported around the body? (13.2)
82 How does exercise affect the exchanges taking place within the body? (13.3)
85 How do exchanges in the kidney help us to maintain the internal environment in mammals and how has biology helped us to treat kidney disease? (13.4)
88 How are microorganisms used to make food and drink? (13.5)
90 What other useful substances can we make using microorganisms? (13.6)
93 How can we be sure we are using microorganisms safely? (13.7)
94 Key Words

The numbers in brackets correspond to the reference numbers on the AQA GCSE Biology specification.

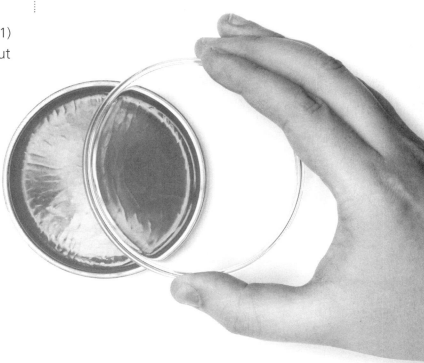

How Science Works

The following questions are designed to make sure you understand what the How Science Works element of your AQA GCSE science course is all about.

1 Only one statement in each of the following sets is accurate. Read them all carefully and then place a tick beside the correct one.

a) i) The term 'How Science Works' refers to a set of key concepts. ☐

   ii) The term 'How Science Works' refers to a set of unanswered questions. ☐

   iii) The term 'How Science Works' refers to a set of scientific facts. ☐

b) i) How Science Works is only relevant to biology. ☐

   ii) How Science Works is relevant to all areas of science. ☐

   iii) How science works only refers to past scientific work. ☐

c) i) How Science Works is normally taught separately. ☐

   ii) How Science Works is normally taught alongside the science content. ☐

   iii) How Science Works is not taught in the classroom. ☐

d) i) There will be no questions relating to How Science Works in the exam. ☐

   ii) There will be a separate exam covering How Science Works. ☐

   iii) In the exam you will need to recall facts and draw upon your knowledge of how science works. ☐

2 Use the words below to fill the spaces and complete this list, which outlines the main areas covered by How Science Works.

society   practices   reliability   explanations
     decisions   procedures   evidence   validity

a) The _____ and _____ used to collect scientific evidence.

b) The relationship between scientific _____ and scientific _____ and theories.

c) The _____ and _____ of scientific evidence.

d) How _____ are made about the use of science and technology.

e) The role of science in _____ .

How Science Works

What is the Purpose of Science?

1 Below are ten statements about science. Read them carefully and then place a tick alongside the ones that are correct.

a) Scientific understanding can lead to the development of new technologies. ☐

b) Science looks for solutions to problems. ☐

c) Science is unconcerned with facts and evidence. ☐

d) Science tries to determine how and why things happen. ☐

e) Scientific knowledge has little relevance in the modern world. ☐

f) Scientific breakthroughs can have a huge impact on society. ☐

g) Scientific knowledge is only useful if you work in medicine. ☐

h) Science attempts to explain the world we live in. ☐

i) Scientific discoveries can impact on the environment. ☐

j) Science does not affect our everyday lives. ☐

Scientific Evidence

2 In your own words, describe the purpose of scientific evidence.

_____
_____
_____

3 Scientific evidence is often based on data. Name two methods of collecting data.

a) _____ b) _____

4 It is important for scientific evidence to be reliable and valid.

a) What is meant by the term 'reliable'? _____

b) What is meant by the term 'valid'? _____

c) *Data can be valid, even if it is not reliable.* Is this statement **true** or **false**? _____

d) Why does data need to be reliable and valid?

_____
_____
_____

How Science Works

Observations

1 The following phrases all refer to important stages in scientific research. Number them **1** to **6**, to show the order in which they normally take place.

a) Analyse the data ☐

b) Develop a hypothesis ☐

c) Make an observation ☐

d) Amend the hypothesis ☐

e) Carry out an investigation ☐

f) Make a prediction ☐

2 a) Write **true** or **false**, as appropriate, alongside each of these statements about hypotheses.

i) A hypothesis summarises a number of related observations. _____

ii) A hypothesis is a statement which suggests an explanation for something. _____

iii) A hypothesis is a question which asks why a phenomenon occurs. _____

iv) A hypothesis normally proposes a relationship between two variables. _____

v) A hypothesis is a conclusion based on scientific data. _____

b) What are hypotheses based on?

_____

3 What must happen if new observations, and related data, do not match existing theories and explanations relating to the same phenomenon?

_____

How Science Works

Investigations

1 What is the purpose of a scientific investigation?

2 In a scientific investigation there are two variables: the independent variable and the dependent variable. In the space below, write a short definition for each to help you remember the difference.

a) Independent variable

b) Dependent variable

3 A student predicts that water will evaporate at a faster rate if room temperature is increased.

For his investigation he places a beaker containing water in three different rooms. Each room is kept at a different temperature: 15°C, 20°C and 25°C.

He measures the amount of water remaining in each beaker every 24 hours.

a) Which is the independent variable in this investigation? Explain your answer.

b) Which is the dependent variable in this investigation? Explain your answer.

c) Is the dependent variable **continuous**, **discrete**, **ordered** or **categoric**?

d) Identify one other variable that could affect the results of this investigation.

How Science Works

Investigations (cont.)

4 For each example below, state whether the link between the two variables, x and y, is **causal**, **due to association**, or **due to chance**.

a) Variables x and y appear to be related, because an increase in x coincides with an increase in y. However, a scientific investigation finds that they are both acting independently.

b) Variables x and y both start to decrease at the same time. A scientific investigation finds that the decreases in x and y are both the result of an increase in variable z.

c) A scientific investigation finds that a change in variable x brings about a change in variable y.

5 a) What is a fair test?

b) In general terms, how can you ensure a fair test?

c) Why is it often easier to achieve a fair test in laboratory conditions than in the field (e.g. when carrying out an investigation into the effects of pollutants on the environment)?

6 When conducting a scientific survey, why is it important to ensure that the individuals in the sample are closely matched?

How Science Works

Investigations (cont.)

7 The following passage describes how a control experiment can be used in a scientific investigation. The words **dependent**, **independent** and **data** have been deleted. Insert them into the correct spaces to complete the passage.

Scientists collect _____ by carrying out investigations. For example, they might set up an experiment in which they can make controlled changes to the _____ variable and then measure the _____ variable.

In a control experiment, the _____ variable is not changed, but the _____ variable is still measured. This provides a second set of _____ .

By comparing the two sets of _____ , the investigator can establish whether changes to the _____ variable were caused by the _____ variable.

If the _____ variable shows the same changes in the control experiment, then they cannot have been caused by the _____ variable.

8 a) In an investigation, why is it a good idea to repeat the measurements and then calculate their mean?

_____

_____

b) What is the standard formula for calculating the mean of a set of measurements?

_____

c) Calculate the mean of the following set of data (show your working).

	Temperature (°C)
1	45.2
2	44.8
3	44.7
4	45.0
5	44.7

Answer: _____

How Science Works

Measurements

1) Name three factors that can affect the reliability and validity of measurements.

a) ....

b) ....

c) ....

2) A student repeats the same measurement ten times. She notices that one of the readings is very different from the rest of the data. In your own words, explain what she should do next.

....

....

....

Presenting Data

3) Name two benefits of presenting data in an appropriate graph or chart.

a) ....

b) ....

4) A meteorologist measures the air temperature in degrees Celsius (°C) every 60 minutes. What type of graph could best be used to display this data? Explain your answer.

....

....

Conclusions

5) Write **true** or **false**, as appropriate, alongside each of the following statements about scientific conclusions.

Conclusions should…

a) include speculation and personal opinion. ....

b) describe the patterns and relationships shown in the data. ....

c) take all the data into account. ....

d) only refer to the bits of data that support the hypothesis. ....

e) make direct reference to the original hypothesis. ....

How Science Works

Conclusions (cont.)

6 Name three points that need to be considered in an evaluation.

a) ....

b) ....

c) ....

7 Suggest one way in which the reliability of an investigation can be improved.

....

8 Use a line to connect each type of issue with the area it is concerned with.

Social Issues		Money and resources
Economic Issues		Morals and value judgements
Environmental Issues		The human population
Ethical Issues		The Earth's ecosystems

9 a) List the three things you should always consider when asked to evaluate information about social-scientific issues.

i) P..................... ii) M..................... iii) I.....................

b) Name three factors that could influence the reliability of information about social-scientific issues.

i) .... ii) .... iii) ....

10 *Science can answer all questions.* Is this statement **true** or **false**? Explain your answer.

....

....

....

....

Unit 1 – 11.1

The Nervous System

1 Name the four main components (parts) of the nervous system:

a) .... b) ....

c) .... d) ....

2 Identify the parts of the nervous system shown on the the diagram alongside.

a) ....

b) ....

c) ....

Neurones

3 Neurones are an important part of the nervous system.

a) What is a neurone?

....

b) What is the main function of a neurone?

....

c) Name two ways in which the structure of a neurone helps it to perform this function.

i) ....

ii) ....

Connections Between Neurones

4 Fill in the missing words to complete the passage below, which describes what happens when an electrical impulse reaches the gap between neurones.

An electrical impulse travels down Neurone A until it reaches the gap, called a ....

Neurone A releases a .... This travels across the gap and activates

.... on Neurone B. In Neurone B, an .... is generated.

The .... is immediately destroyed.

Unit 1 – 11.1

Types of Receptor

1 There are receptors all over the human body. For each location given below, name one type of stimulus that the receptors found there detect. The first one has been completed for you.

a) Eyes ____**Light**____   b) Nose _____   c) Ears _____

d) Skin _____   e) Tongue _____

Conscious Action

2 Use the words provided to complete the flow chart and show the pathway for receiving information and then acting upon it.

Response	Receptors	Effectors	Stimulus	Coordinator
a)	b)	c)	d)	e)

Reflex Action

3 What is the main purpose of a reflex action? _____

4 In terms of the pathway, explain the main difference between a conscious action and a reflex action.

_____

_____

_____

5 Number the following descriptions **1** to **5**, to show the sequence of events that occur when you touch a hot object.

a) The muscles in the arm contract, pulling the hand away from the hot object. ☐

b) An impulse passes along a sensory neurone to the spinal cord. ☐

c) A receptor in the hand is stimulated by the hot object. ☐

d) The relay neurone synapses with a motor neurone, sending impulses down it. ☐

e) The sensory neurone synapses with a relay neurone, bypassing the brain. ☐

Unit 1 – 11.1

Internal Conditions

1 The human body needs to maintain relatively constant levels of temperature, water, ions and blood sugar.

a) Why does human body temperature need to be maintained at approximately 37°C? ....

b) Name three ways in which water is removed from the body.

   i) ....   **ii)** ....   **iii)** ....

c) How does the body take on ions? ....

d) Why does the body need glucose? ....

2 Hormones play an important role in maintaining the body's internal conditions.

a) Where are hormones produced? ....

b) How are hormones transported to their target organs? ....

Hormones and Fertility

3 The hormones that control female fertility are produced in two places. Name both of these places.

a) ....   **b)** ....

4 For each hormone named below, use an arrow to show which explanation best describes its function.

a) Oestrogen	Stimulates the ovaries so that an egg matures and oestrogen is produced.
b) LH	Triggers the release of a mature egg.
c) FSH	Makes the pituitary gland stop producing FSH and begin producing LH.

5 a) Which hormone can be given to women increase their fertility?

....

b) Which hormone can be given to women to reduce their fertility?

....

How Science Works

To answer the questions on this page, you will have to recall scientific facts and draw upon your knowledge of how science works, e.g. scientific procedures, issues and ideas.

1 The following information appears on the label of a bottle of energy drink:

> This drink contains glucose, fluids and ions (sodium) for maximum performance during exercise.

a) What does the body use glucose for?

b) Why might the body need a higher intake of glucose before or during exercise?

c) Name three ways in which water can be lost from the body.

   i)

   ii)

   iii)

d) During exercise, the amount of water lost by two of these methods increases. Name both these methods.

   i) .... ii) ....

e) How does the body lose ions like sodium?

f) Based on your answers in parts **a)** to **e)**, do you think this sports drink could benefit an athlete if drunk before or during training? Explain your answer.

How Science Works

To answer the questions on this page, you will have to recall scientific facts and draw upon your knowledge of how science works, e.g. scientific procedures, issues and ideas.

1. FSH is sometimes given to women who are finding it difficult to conceive. What effect does FSH have on the female body?

2. Name one situation where FSH would not help to improve a couple's chance of getting pregnant.

3. Give one reason why an infertile couple might prefer to try IVF treatment rather than adopt a baby.

4. Give one reason why an infertile couple might adopt a baby rather than try IVF treatment.

5. Below is some additional information about IVF treatment:

   > In normal pregnancies, no more than 2% of women have a multiple birth, e.g. give birth to twins, triplets, etc. With IVF treatment, the chance of having a multiple birth rises to 25%. Most multiple births are twins, but higher multiple births are on the increase.

   a) Describe one problem a multiple birth might cause for a couple.

   b) If IVF treatment becomes more common, the number of multiple births will increase. What effect could this potentially have on the size of the population?

   c) Give one reason why this might have a negative impact on society.

Unit 1 – 11.2

Metabolic Rate

1 What does the term 'metabolic rate' refer to?

2 Read the statements below. Use a tick to indicate which three factors can affect an individual's metabolic rate.

a) The amount of fatty foods they eat ☐

b) Genes inherited from their parents ☐

c) The amount of water they drink ☐

d) The amount of physical activity they do ☐

e) The ratio of fat to muscle in their body ☐

f) Their hair colour ☐

3 a) What is the cause of malnourishment?

b) Describe one way in which you might recognise someone as being malnourished?

4 Unscramble the letters below to find five things that are essential in a balanced diet.

a) BRIEF

b) REALMSIN

c) SINAMVIT

d) PINROTE

e) HOBARTDARCEY

5 What is meant by a 'balanced' diet?

6 The risk of heart disease is increased if you are overweight. Name two other diseases that are linked to excess weight.

a)   b)

7 In your own words, explain why the diseases in Question 6 are more common in the UK and America than in many African countries.

Unit 1 – 11.2

How to Improve the Diet

1) A high cholesterol level can cause health problems.

   a) Where in the body is cholesterol produced? ....

   b) What two factors influence how much cholesterol an individual's liver produces?

   i) .... **ii)** ....

2) Cholesterol is transported around the body by lipoproteins.

   a) What is a lipoprotein?

   ....

   b) There are two types of lipoprotein. What is the name given to the variety that can cause health problems?

   ....

3) Why is it important not to eat too much salt?

   ....

4) Why is it better to prepare your own food from fresh ingredients than to use ready-made processed meals?

   ....

   ....

5) Jennie's dad has been told that he has high cholesterol and high blood pressure.

   a) Use a tick to indicate which type(s) of food he can eat to help him lower his cholesterol level.

   i) Saturated fat ☐   **iii)** Low-density lipoproteins ☐

   ii) Polyunsaturated fat ☐   **iv)** Monounsaturated fat ☐

   b) At the supermarket, he has to choose between the products listed below. For each pair, put a ring around the option he should buy to help improve his diet.

   i) Butter or sunflower margarine   **iv)** Skimmed milk or full-fat milk

   ii) Tuna steak or beef steak   **v)** New potatoes or oven chips

   iii) Salted peanuts or unsalted peanuts

How Science Works

To answer the questions on this page, you will have to recall scientific facts and draw upon your knowledge of how science works, e.g. scientific procedures, issues and ideas.

1 Read this information about monosodium glutamate and then answer the questions below.

> Monosodium glutamate (MSG) contains an amino acid that is naturally occurring in most foods, especially those that are high in proteins like meat and fish. It is also added to many savoury foods by manufacturers as a flavour enhancer.
>
> However, although the amino acid is needed by the human body for a variety of functions, it is not essential to a balanced diet because the human body produces its own supply.
>
> In the EU, MSG is classified as a food additive (E621) and its use is regulated. However, many people believe that food additives like this shouldn't be used at all.
>
> MSG has no particular flavour or texture of its own. It contains one-third of the amount of sodium of table salt, and far less is required to achieve the same flavour-enhancing results. In some other countries, MSG is used as a seasoning in the same way that we use salt and pepper.
>
> Some people believe that MSG can cause symptoms that include a burning sensation on the back of the neck, a tight chest, nausea and sweating. This complaint has been dubbed 'Chinese Restaurant Syndrome' because MSG is commonly used in Asian cooking. Other studies have linked MSG to eyesight deterioration. However, no research has produced reliable evidence to support claims that MSG is the cause of either of these conditions.

a) A scientist performs tests on a sample of food and discovers that it contains the amino acid found in monosodium glutamate. Give two possible explanations for this.

i) ....

ii) ....

b) Is it necessary to include MSG in a balanced diet? Explain your answer.

....

....

c) The use of MSG as a food additive is controversial.

i) Give one argument against its use.

....

ii) Give one argument supporting its use.

....

How Science Works

To answer the questions on this page, you will have to recall scientific facts and draw upon your knowledge of how science works, e.g. scientific procedures, issues and ideas.

1) You are asked to design a poster to encourage a healthy lifestyle.

State two key points that you would include on your poster.

a) _____

b) _____

2) A new diet claims to result in rapid weight loss by boosting the body's metabolic rate.

a) What does the term 'metabolic rate' refer to?

_____

b) Are the foods you eat likely to have an immediate effect on your metabolic rate? Explain your answer.

_____
_____
_____
_____

c) Suggest a more effective way to increase metabolic rate.

_____
_____

d) Could your answer to part **c)**, result in weight loss? Explain your answer.

_____
_____
_____
_____

3) Some diets tell you to cut out a whole food group, e.g. carbohydrates or fats. Why is this a bad idea?

_____
_____

Unit 1 – 11.3

Drugs

1 Write a short definition for the word 'drug'.

_____

2 Fill in the missing words to complete this passage about drugs.

Some drugs are obtained from _____ substances. Others are synthetic, which means they are _____ .

Drugs can have _____ qualities, but they can also be harmful.

Before drugs are trialled using volunteers, they are tested in the laboratory for _____ .

Developing New Drugs

3 For each statement below, indicate the correct option by placing a tick beside it.

a) Thalidomide was approved as a…

   i) cure for cancer. ☐   **ii)** sleeping pill. ☐   **iii)** painkiller. ☐

b) Thalidomide was then found to relieve…

   i) morning sickness. ☐   **ii)** travel sickness. ☐   **iii)** altitude sickness. ☐

c) Many babies born to mothers who took Thalidomide had…

   i) brain damage. ☐   **ii)** poor eye sight. ☐   **iii)** limb abnormalities. ☐

d) The Thalidomide example highlights the importance of…

   i) comprehensive drug testing. ☐   **ii)** genetic testing. ☐   **iii)** developing new drugs. ☐

e) Thalidomide is now used to treat…

   i) morning sickness. ☐   **ii)** insomnia. ☐   **iii)** leprosy. ☐

Unit 1 – 11.3

Legal and Illegal Drugs

1) Both legal and illegal drugs get used for recreational purposes.

a) Name two legal drugs that are used recreationally.

i) .... ii) ....

b) Name two illegal drugs that are used recreationally.

i) .... ii) ....

2) Some drugs are addictive. Name one commonly used, legal drug that is highly addictive.

....

3) Below are some of the withdrawal symptoms suffered by addicts when they stop using a drug. Arrange them in the table depending on whether they are psychological or physical.

paranoia   sweating   shaking   vomiting   diarrhoea   depression   cravings   anxiety

Psychological Symptoms	Physical Symptoms

4) Alcohol is a depressant.

a) What effect does a depressant have on the body?

....

b) What are the possible consequences of excessive alcohol consumption?

....

c) Which two organs can be permanently damaged as a result of long-term alcohol consumption?

i) .... ii) ....

How Science Works

To answer the questions on this page, you will have to recall scientific facts and draw upon your knowledge of how science works, e.g. scientific procedures, issues and ideas.

1 High levels of cholesterol can lead to heart attacks.

   a) What does LDL stand for? _____

   b) What is atherosclerosis? _____

   c) In your own words, explain how LDLs can lead to atherosclerosis.

   _____
   _____
   _____

   d) Name two symptoms that a person having a heart attack might display.

   i) _____ ii) _____

2 Statins are drugs that are given to people who have high cholesterol levels which have not been successfully controlled by changes in diet.

   a) Describe briefly how statins lower LDL levels.

   _____
   _____
   _____

   b) Give one related benefit of taking statins.

   _____

   c) List three side effects that can be caused by statins.

   i) _____

   ii) _____

   iii) _____

   d) Give one other drawback associated with taking statins.

   _____

How Science Works

To answer the questions on this page, you will have to recall scientific facts and draw upon your knowledge of how science works, e.g. scientific procedures, issues and ideas.

1 Some drugs are legal whilst others are illegal.

a) What is a drug?

b) Why is it important to test drugs under laboratory conditions?

c) Why is it important to test drugs on human volunteers?

d) Why do you think some drugs are illegal?

2 Cocaine is an illegal, Class A drug. However, some people choose to use it recreationally.

a) Suggest one reason why someone might take cocaine.

b) Name two physical effects of taking cocaine.

i) ii)

c) Fill in the missing words to complete the passage below.

Cocaine is very _____. People can become psychologically _____ on the feelings it produces. It is also _____ addictive; with regular use, the body starts to need the drug. If an addict stops taking the drug, they get _____.

d) In your own words, complete the following sentence:

A cocaine addiction might lead to financial problems because…

STUDENT WORKBOOK ANSWERS

The Essentials of GCSE
AQA **biology**
Edited by R. Skinner

Ordering Details

INFORMATION

For up-to-date product information, including prices, please visit our website or telephone our customer services department:

Web: www.lonsdalesrg.co.uk
Enquiries: 015395 65921

EDUCATIONAL PROVIDERS

Educational providers can order on-line and by fax, telephone or post:

Lonsdale, Westmorland House, Elmsfield Park, Holme, Carnforth Lancashire LA6 1RJ

Order Line: 015395 65920
Fax: 015395 64167
Web: www.lonsdalesrg.co.uk

PRIVATE CUSTOMERS

Secure ordering is available on-line at **www.lonsdalesrg.co.uk**

www.lonsdalesrg.co.uk
Browse for a full list of publications and further information

Page 4

1. **a)** i) The term 'How Science Works' refers to a set of key concepts. ✓
   b) ii) How Science Works is relevant to all areas of science. ✓
   c) ii) How Science Works is normally taught alongside the science content. ✓
   d) iii) In the exam, you will need to recall facts and draw upon your knowledge of how science works. ✓

2. **a)** practices, procedures
   b) evidence, explanations
   c) reliability, validity
   d) decisions
   e) society

Page 5

1. **a)** ✓ **b)** ✓ **c)** ✗ **d)** ✓ **e)** ✗ **f)** ✓ **g)** ✗ **h)** ✓ **i)** ✓ **j)** ✗

2. The purpose of scientific evidence is to provide facts which answer a specific question, and therefore support or disprove an idea or theory.

3. **In any order: a)** Observations. **b)** Measurements.

4. **a)** It must be reproducible by others and must therefore be trustworthy.
   b) It must be reliable and it must answer the question.
   c) False.
   d) To allow scientists to reach appropriate conclusions.

Page 6

1. **a)** Stage 5 **b)** Stage 2 **c)** Stage 1 **d)** Stage 6 **e)** Stage 4 **f)** Stage 3

2. **a) i)** False **ii)** True **iii)** False **iv)** True **v)** False
   b) Observations, scientific knowledge and creative thinking.

3. They need to be checked for reliability and validity.

Page 7

1. To try to determine whether there is a relationship between two variables.

2. **a)** An independent variable is controlled or known by the person carrying out the investigation.
   b) A dependent variable is measured each time a change is made to the independent variable to see if it also changes.

3. **a)** The room temperature, because it is controlled by the student.
   b) The volume of water remaining in the beaker after 24 hours, because it is dependent on room temperature (the independent variable).
   c) Continuous
   d) Accept any suitable answer, e.g. the amount of water in each beaker at the start of the investigation.

Page 8

4. **a)** due to chance **b)** due to association **c)** causal

5. **a)** A fair test is one in which the only factor that can affect the dependent variable is the independent variable.
   b) All other variables that could affect the dependent variable must be kept the same.
   c) Because it is easier to control conditions such as temperature, light intensity, etc.

6. To reduce the impact of outside variables.

Page 9

7. data, independent, dependent, independent, dependent, data, data, dependent, independent, dependent, independent

8. **a)** To overcome small variations and get a best estimate of the true value. Increasing the number of measurements taken will improve the accuracy and reliability.
   b) Mean = $\dfrac{\text{Sum of all measurements}}{\text{Number of measurements}}$
   c) $\dfrac{224.4}{5} = 44.88°C$ (2 d.p.)

Page 10

1. **In any order:**
   a) Accuracy of instruments used.
   b) Sensitivity of instruments used.
   c) Human error.

2. She should try to find out whether it was caused by an equipment failure or human error. If so, she should discount them from any following calculations.

3. **In any order:**
   a) It makes it easier to see the relationship between two variables.
   b) It makes it easy to identify any anomalous values.

4. Line graph, because both variables are continuous.

5. **a)** False
   b) True
   c) True
   d) False
   e) True

Page 11

6. **a), b) and c) Accept any three from:** the original purpose of the investigation; the appropriateness of the methods and techniques used; the reliability and validity of the data; the validity of the conclusions.

7. **Accept any one from:** looking at relevant data from secondary sources; using an alternative method to check results; ensuring that the results can be reproduced by others.

8. Social Issues – The human population
   Economic Issues – Money and resources
   Environmental Issues – The Earth's ecosystems
   Ethical Issues – Morals and value judgements

9. **a) i)** Pluses **ii)** Minuses **iii)** Impact on society
   b) In any order: i) Opinion **ii)** Bias **iii)** Weight of evidence

10. False. Science cannot answer some questions because there is not enough reliable and valid evidence, and it cannot provide answers to ethical questions.

Page 12

1. **In any order: a)** Brain **b)** Spinal cord **c)** Spinal nerves **d)** Receptors

2. **a)** Brain **b)** Spinal cord **c)** Spinal nerves

3. **a)** A specially adapted, elongated cell which carries information from receptors to the brain.
   b) They carry an electrical signal, e.g. a nerve impulse (from receptors to the brain to the effectors).
   c) Accept any two of the following, in any order:
   They are elongated to make connections between parts of the body; They have branches endings which allow a single neurone to act on many muscle fibres; The cell body has many connections to allow communication with lots of other neurones.

4. synapse, chemical transmitter, receptors, electrical impulse, chemical transmitter

Page 13

1. **a)** Light.
   b) Smell.
   c) Sound or change of position.
   d) Touch, pain, pressure or temperature.
   e) Taste.

2. **a)** Stimulus **b)** Receptors **c)** Coordinator **d)** Effectors **e)** Response

3. To prevent harm to the body.

4. A reflex action misses out the brain completely, in order to speed up the response time. The spinal cord acts as the coordinator and passes impulses directly from a sensory neurone to a motor neurone via a relay neurone, which bypasses the brain.

5. **a)** 5 **b)** 2 **c)** 1 **d)** 4 **e)** 3

Page 14

1. **a)** Because that is the temperature at which most body enzymes work best.
   b) In any order: i) Breathing **ii)** Sweating **iii)** In urine.
   c) By eating and drinking.
   d) Glucose provides the cells with a constant supply of energy.

2. **a)** The (endocrine) glands. **b)** By the bloodstream.

3. **In any order: a)** Pituitary gland. **b)** Ovaries.

4. a) Oestrogen – Makes the pituitary gland stop producing FSH and begin producing LH.
   b) LH – Triggers the release of a mature egg.
   c) FSH – Stimulates the ovaries so that an egg matures and oestrogen is produced.
5. a) FSH
   b) Oestrogen

Page 15

1. a) For energy – glucose provides the cells with a constant supply of energy.
   b) Because more energy will be / has been used up.
   c) **In any order: i)** Sweating **ii)** Breathing **iii)** In urine.
   d) **In any order: i)** Sweating **ii)** Breathing.
   e) Ions are lost through sweating, and excess ions are lost via the kidneys in urine.
   f) **Accept any suitable answer with good reasons, e.g.** Yes. Glucose is needed for energy and more energy is used up during exercise. Ions and water are lost through sweating, and sweating increases during exercise. This sports drink could be used to replace the glucose, water and ions that are lost.

Page 16

1. FSH causes the ovaries to produce oestrogen and an egg to mature.
2. **Accept any suitable answer, e.g.** when the problem is a low sperm count; the woman has a blocked oviduct.
3. **Accept any suitable answer, e.g.** because it will be their biological child (have their genes); the woman wants to experience pregnancy and child birth.
4. **Accept any suitable answer, e.g.** IVF can be expensive, emotionally and physically demanding; IVF has a low success rate; there are age restrictions in place for IVF treatment.
5. a) **Accept any suitable answer, e.g.** two or more babies are more demanding and more expensive.
   b) The population size will increase.
   c) **Accept any sensible answer e.g.** increased demand for resources like food; more housing needed; not enough jobs – possible increase in unemployment.

Page 17

1. The rate at which all the chemical reactions in the cells of the body are carried out.
2. a) ✓ b) ✓ c) ✗ d) ✓ e) ✓ f) ✗
3. a) An unbalanced diet.
   b) **Accept either:**
   They are too fat or too thin.
   They have deficiency diseases such as scurvy.
4. a) Fibre b) Minerals c) Vitamins d) Protein e) Carbohydrate
5. A balanced diet incorporates all the different foods your body needs in the correct proportions.
6. **In any order:**
   a) Diabetes b) Arthritis
   Accept any other sensible answer.
7. Because there is more food available, and much of it is high in fat, salt and sugar, people in the UK and America are more likely to become obese than people living in many African countries. This is compounded by the fact that most people in the UK and America do too little exercise (are less likely to do physical work).

Page 18

1. a) The liver.
   b) **In any order: i)** Diet **ii)** Inheritance
2. a) A chemical made of fat (lipid) and protein, which carries cholesterol around the body.
   b) Low-density lipoproteins.
3. Too much salt can lead to high blood pressure.
4. Processed food often contains a high proportion of salt and/or fat. Preparing your own food from ingredients means that you can control what goes into it.
5. a) i) ✗ ii) ✓ iii) ✗ iv) ✓
   b) i) Sunflower margarine.
      ii) Tuna steak.
      iii) Unsalted peanuts.
      iv) Skimmed milk.
      v) New potatoes.

Page 19

1. a) **In any order:**
   i) It is naturally occurring in many foods.
   ii) It is added to many savoury foods by manufacturers as a flavour enhancer.
   b) No, because the human body produces its own supply.
   c) i) **Accept any sensible answer, e.g.** some people believe it can cause symptoms such as nausea and a tight chest; it is a non-essential additive.
   ii) **Accept any sensible answer, e.g.** it occurs naturally in some foods anyway, so it is not harmful; it improves the flavour of foods.

Page 20

1. a) and b) **Accept any suitable points, e.g.** Eat a balanced diet; Exercise regularly; Eat less salt.
2. a) The rate at which the chemical reactions in the body's cells are carried out.
   b) Not an immediate effect, but the foods you eat will eventually have an effect, because metabolic rate is affected by the proportion of fat to muscle in the body.
   c) Exercise regularly.
   d) Yes, because the metabolic rate increases with the amount of exercise you do and stays high for some time after you finish exercising. It can also help to burn fat and develop muscle tissue, favourably changing the ratio of fat to muscle in your body.
3. Because all the food groups are required for a healthy balanced diet.

Page 21

1. A drug is a chemical substance which alters the way the body works.
2. natural, man-made, beneficial, toxicity
3. a) ii) A sleeping pill.
   b) i) Morning sickness.
   c) iii) Limb abnormalities.
   d) i) Comprehensive drug testing.
   e) iii) Leprosy.

Page 22

1. **In any order: a)** Alcohol **b)** Tobacco
   Accept any other suitable answer.
   b) **In any order: a)** Heroin **b)** Cocaine
   Accept any other suitable answer.
2. Tobacco (nicotine).
3. Psychological – paranoia, depression, cravings, anxiety.
   Physical – sweating, shaking, vomiting, diarrhoea.
4. a) It causes reactions to slow down.
   b) Unconsciousness, coma or death.
   c) **In any order: i)** The liver **ii)** The brain.

Page 23

1. a) Low-density lipoproteins.
   b) The narrowing and hardening of the arteries.
   c) High levels of LDLs can cause a build up of a thick fatty substance in the arteries. This causes the arteries to thicken and harden (atherosclerosis).
   d) **In any order: i)** Breathing difficulties **ii)** Chest pain.
2. a) Statins work in the liver to reduce the manufacture of cholesterol.
   b) They reduce LDL levels, and therefore the risk of heart disease or stroke caused by cardio-vascular disease by up to a third.
   c) i), ii) and iii) **Accept any three from:** headaches, sickness, diarrhoea, insomnia, liver problems, stomach upset, hepatitis, muscle aches.

d) **Accept any suitable answer, e.g.** can have unwanted side effects; they must be taken for life; they do not encourage users to adopt a healthier lifestyle.

Page 24

1. a) A drug is a chemical substance which alters how the body works.
    b) They need to be tested in a controlled environment for toxicity before they can be given to humans.
    c) To discover any side effects (and check they are effective).
    d) **Accept any suitable answer, e.g.** Because they are toxic; they have extreme side effects; they have not been properly tested in controlled conditions.

2. a) **Accept any suitable answer, e.g.** For social confidence; peer-group pressure.
    b) **In any order: i)** Raises heart rate **ii)** Raises blood pressure.
    c) addictive, dependent, physically, withdrawal symptoms.
    d) **Accept any suitable answer, e.g.** Cocaine is very expensive, and the more you have, the more you need. Addicts can end up getting into debt to fund their habit.

Page 25

1. **In any order: a)** Carcinogens **b)** Tar

2. Tar – can lead to bronchitis, emphysema and lung cancer.
   OR Carcinogens – can cause cancer.

3. **a) and b) Accept two, in any order:** Mental illness; Fainting (disruption of blood pressure); Psychologically addictive.
   Accept any other suitable answers.

4. **Accept any suitable answer, e.g.** the nicotine in tobacco is addictive.

5. **a) and b) Accept two, in any order:** Cancer; Multiple sclerosis; HIV.
   Accept any other suitable answers.

6. a) That it can lead to more addictive and harmful drugs such as heroin and cocaine.
    b) Because many cannabis smokers never go on to use any harder drugs.

7. **Accept any suitable answer, e.g.** Because the drug has been downgraded people might perceive it to be less harmful. This could lead to more users, who could potentially go on to try other illegal drugs.

Page 26

1. a) **In any order: i)** Pollution **ii)** Tar (used in new roads).
    b) The Medical Research Council.
    c) They found a strong correlation between heavy smoking and lung cancer.

2.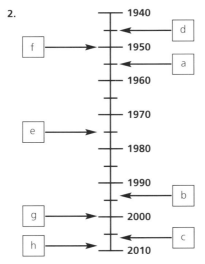

Page 27

1. The nicotine in tobacco is mentally and physically addictive, so they will experience severe withdrawal symptoms and cravings. The act of smoking will also have become a habit, so they will have to change their patterns of behaviour.

2. Nicotine replacement products – This helps relieve the withdrawal symptoms and cravings, helping you to break the psychological habit.
   Hypnotherapy – This helps you deal with the emotional and psychological aspects of quitting smoking.
   Acupuncture – This stimulates pressure points on the body and helps to alleviate withdrawal symptoms.
   Cold turkey – This relies entirely on willpower to stop.

3. a) i), ii) and iii) **Accept any suitable answers, e.g.** It can be used to help give up smoking; it is suitable for heavy smokers; it alleviates many of the withdrawal symptoms.
    b) i), ii) and iii) **Accept any suitable answers, e.g.** It is not suitable for people with a history of fits or eating disorders; it should not be used during pregnancy; side effects include insomnia, a dry mouth and headaches.

Page 28

1. A microorganism that causes an infectious disease.

2. **a) and b) Accept two, in any order:** tetanus, TB, cholera.
   Accept any other suitable answers.

3. **a) and b) Accept two, in any order:** colds, flu, measles, polio.
   Accept any other suitable answers.

4. **In any order:**
   a) They ingest pathogens, producing antitoxins to neutralise toxins produced by the pathogens.
   b) They produce antibodies to destroy particular pathogens.

5. painkillers, kill (or destroy), bacteria, viruses, reproduce.

6. **a)** 2 **b)** 5 **c)** 3 **d)** 1 **e)** 4

Page 29

1. Germs (microorganisms) could get onto doctors' hands and be passed between patients, spreading infection. By washing their hands between patients, doctors get rid of most of these germs so that infections cannot be spread as easily.

2. The 19th century.

3. **Poster should include five of the following key points:** Hands must be washed between dealing with patients; All surgical instruments must be sterilised; All wards must be cleaned thoroughly; All spillages must be cleared up immediately; All patients with infectious diseases must be isolated; disposable face masks, gowns and gloves must be worn.

Page 30

1. a) **i)** Virus **ii)** Virus **iii)** Bacteria **iv)** Bacteria **v)** Bacteria
    b) They are caused by bacteria which means they can be treated using antibiotics. In the 19th century, these antibiotics had not been developed. In addition, we now have a better understanding of how infections are spread so preventative measures can be taken. There is also a vaccine against TB.
    c) Measles and mumps are caused by viruses, which means that they cannot be treated using antibiotics.

2. a) A virus.
    b) It could mutate into a strain that could be passed between humans.

Page 31

1. a) **i)** Diphtheria – Upper respiratory tract and skin – sore throat, headache, fever, rapid pulse, swollen neck glands.
       ii) Tetanus – Wounded part of body / muscles nearest wound – muscle spasms, rapid heartbeat, fever, diarrhoea, sore throat.
       iii) Polio – Gastro-intestinal tract – fever, sore throat, headache, vomiting, fatigue, stiffness of neck and back, tiredness.
    b) **In any order:**
       i) It protects against diphtheria, tetanus and polio.
       ii) It is free to all UK residents.
    c) **In any order:**
       i) There are possible side effects.
       ii) It can have adverse effects if given to people who have been vaccinated against diphtheria or tetanus within the last 5 years.

Page 32

1. **a)** ii) ✓ **b)** i) ✓ **c)** iii) ✓

2. **a)** Disease **b)** Migration **c)** Predation **d)** Competition

3. **a)** Space / light **b)** Food **c)** Water

4. a), b) and c) Accept any three from: rounded shape means a small area to volume ratio to reduce heat loss; large amount of insulating fat beneath skin; thick greasy fur to repel water and insulate; white coat for camouflage; large feet to spread weight on ice; powerful swimmer to catch food.

Page 33

1. **a)** Cave
   b) Mangrove Swamp
   c) Rainforest
   d) Desert
   e) Depths of Ocean
   f) Mountain

2. Penguins' streamlined bodies and webbed feet allow them to swim well to catch food. Their thick skin with thick layer of fat insulates the penguins, keeping them warm. They huddle together to share body heat.

3. **a)** This means the animal can be kicked, clawed or bitten by prey (or competitors) with little chance of injury.
   b) This allows them to catch and hold down prey – the large paws are very powerful.
   c) They need to be camouflaged.

Page 34

1. **In any order: a)** Space / light **b)** Water **c)** Food

2. **a)** Beech tree – for light from the Sun for photosynthesis, space in the ground for their roots, nutrients and water from the ground.
   b) Woodlouse / Ground beetle – for food and water, and space to live.
   c) Chaffinch – for space to nest in the trees, for food and water.
   d) There will be few plants living there, because plants require light for photosynthesis. Insects like centipedes and beetles, which favour dark, damp conditions are found in greater numbers in these areas.

Page 35

1.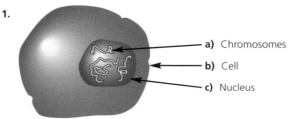
   a) Chromosomes
   b) Cell
   c) Nucleus

2. **a)** Gametes
   b) Chromosomes
   c) Genes

3. **a)** Differences between individuals of the same species.
   b) In any order:
      i) Genetic. Example: hair colour.
      ii) Environmental. Example: weight.
   Accept any other suitable examples.

4. During sexual reproduction, a sperm from a male fuses with an egg from a female, so the genes carried by each are mixed together to produce a new individual. In asexual reproduction, the genes only come from one parent, so variation can only by caused by environmental factors.

Page 36

1. **a)** 3 **b)** 1 **c)** 6 **d)** 4 **e)** 5 **f)** 2

2. Stage 1: Parents with desirable characteristics are mated.
   Stage 2: Embryo is removed before the cells become specialised.
   Stage 3: The embryo is split into several clumps (smaller embryos).
   Stage 4: These embryos are implanted into the uteruses of sheep who give birth to clones.

Page 37

1. organism, early, characteristics, cloned

2. **a) and b) Accept any suitable answers, e.g.** they are redder, bigger, etc.

3.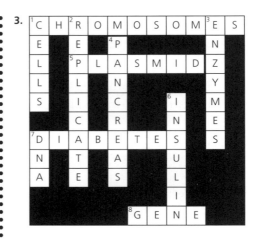

Page 38

1. **Accept any suitable answer, e.g.** Economic argument for GM crops: higher yields can be produced; Economic argument against GM crops: only big GM manufacturers benefit.

2. **Accept any suitable answer, e.g.** Social argument for GM crops: they can be enriched to benefit health; Social argument against GM crops: unknown long term effects on health.

3. **Accept any suitable answer, e.g.** Ethical argument for GM crops: they could be used to help the developing world; Ethical argument against GM crops: farming methods could have a negative impact on the environment and wildlife.

4. **Accept any suitable answer, e.g.** Economic argument for animal cloning: allows quick response to livestock and crop shortages; Economic argument against animal cloning: a public backlash against cloned stock could cause a market crash.

Page 39

1. **c)** ✓

2. **a)** Direct competition from a better adapted species can lead to a reduction in numbers of a species. As the better adapted species reproduces and the population increases, the other species' numbers will dwindle and can eventually lead to extinction.
   b) Changes in the environment such as warming or cooling of temperature may happen too quickly for an organism to adapt, leading eventually to its extinction.

3. Fossils are the remains of plants and animals from many years ago, found in rock. They can show the gradual changes that have taken place over long periods of time, providing strong evidence for evolution.

4. Those which are better adapted to the environment.

5. Better adapted.

6. Mutations.

Page 40

1. **a)** They both believe in the existence of a creator or higher being.
   b) Darwin's theory states that all organisms evolved from simple organisms. The Creationist theory states that each organism was created separately and did not evolve. The Intelligent Design theory states that certain structures within organisms are too sophisticated to be the product of evolution.

2. Darwin believed that characteristics caused by genetic factors could be passed on to offspring. Lamarck believed that variations caused by environmental factors (acquired characteristics) could be passed on to offspring.

3. 19th century society would have been reluctant to accept Darwin's theory because it went against everything they believed, e.g. that God created all living things (the story of Genesis).

4. **Accept any suitable answer, e.g.** it was difficult to prove.

5. **a)** The fossil record provides evidence that organisms have gradually changed (evolved) over long periods of time.
   b) They view the gaps in the fossil record as evidence against evolution.

Page 41

1. a)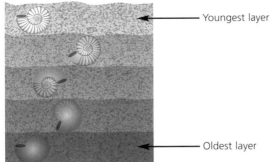
   Youngest layer
   Oldest layer

   b) It shows the gradual change of an organism over many, many years.

2. It means that fossils are not always in chronological order and that some may have been lost.

3. It means that the fossil record is incomplete: very few organisms would have died in the right conditions (silt/mud), producing fossils.

4. It means that the fossil record is incomplete: it cannot provide evidence for the evolution of features such as tentacles and boneless protrusions.

Page 42

1. a) It is increasing with accelerating speed (the larger it gets, the quicker it grows).

   b)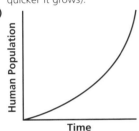

   c) i) and ii) Accept any suitable answers, e.g. people are living for longer; more cures are being developed for diseases.
   d) Because they are non-renewable resources – they cannot be replaced in a lifetime.
   e) i) and ii) Accept any suitable answers, e.g. increased pollution from human activity, like transport and industry; more land is being taken up to use for housing and farming.

2.
   In any order:
   i) Sulfur dioxide
   ii) Carbon dioxide
   iii) Fertiliser
   iv) Pesticide
   v) Smoke
   vi) Nitrogen oxide
   vii) Sewage
   viii) Herbicide

Page 43

1. The large-scale cutting down of trees.

2. In any order:
   a) For timber.
   b) To provide land for agriculture.

3. In any order:
   a) The trees in rainforests take carbon dioxide out of the air – without them carbon dioxide levels in the atmosphere will rise rapidly.
   b) The rainforests are full of different plant and animal species, many of which will become extinct if the rainforest is destroyed, reducing biodiversity.
   c) A lot of the chopped down wood will decompose or be burned, which releases more carbon dioxide into the atmosphere.

4. To improve the quality of life for current generations, without compromising future generations.

5. In any order:
   a) Methane
   b) Carbon dioxide
   Accept any other suitable answers.

6. Greenhouse gases act like an insulating layer around the Earth, preventing too much heat energy from escaping into space. However, because the levels of these gases are increasing, more and more heat is being kept inside, so the overall temperature will gradually increase.

Page 44

1. In any order:
   a) Economic development.
   b) Social development.
   c) Environmental development.

2. c) ✓

3. In any order:
   a) Limiting exploitation by using quotas.
   b) Ensuring the stocks are replenished.
   Accept any other suitable answers.

4. Accept any suitable answer, e.g. Quotas: sea fishing; Replenishment: Scandinavian pine forests.

5. a) Its habitats were destroyed.
   b) Protected sites have been established in Wales where the osprey can live and breed undisturbed.

Page 45

1. The glaciers will begin to melt.

2. a) If the glacier has changed in size over the 10 year period.
   b) That the glacier had increased in size.
   c) That the glacier had decreased in size (melted).
   d) That the glacier is melting at an increasingly faster rate.

Page 46

1. a) In any order:
      i) Measure levels at the same time every day.
      ii) Measure levels in the same place every day.
      Accept any other suitable answer.
   b) i) To obtain reliable and accurate results.
      ii) **Accept any suitable answer, e.g.** different weather conditions; different traffic levels.
      iii) That an error has been made recording this measurement.
      iv) Carbon monoxide levels in the village were much higher before the bypass opened. The bypass has led to a significant reduction in the levels of carbon monoxide in the village.

Page 47

1. a) If there were no fishing quotas, fisherman would be able to catch as much fish as they wanted. This could lead to over-fishing and stocks would soon decrease.
   b) i) **Accept any suitable answer, e.g.** other species' numbers may decrease (predators of the extinct species) and other species' numbers might increase (prey of the extinct species).
      ii) **Accept any suitable answer, e.g.** this may lead to less choice of fish for humans to eat as more and more species' numbers decrease.
   c) quotas, limit, income, boats, decommissioning, economy, tourism.

Page 48

1.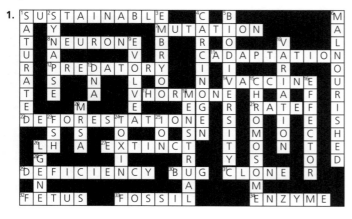

Page 49

1.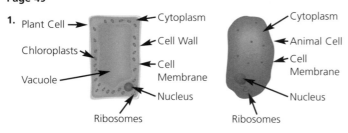

2. a) Cellulose
   b) Nucleus
   c) Chlorophyll
   d) Cell membrane

3.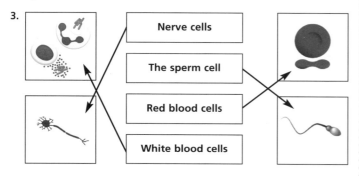

Page 50

1. To enable each cell to perform a specific function.

2. a) cell membrane, nucleus, mitochondria, cytoplasm.
   b) fibres that slide past each other, so it can change length.
   c) i) So that they can stretch, allowing us to move parts of our bodies.
      ii) Mitochondria produce the cells' energy and muscle cells need lots of energy to produce movement.

3. a) **Accept any suitable answer, e.g.** they are more effective when they are in large groups and work together.
   b) **Accept any suitable answer, e.g.** in the nose, in the lungs.

Page 51

1. Because useful substances like glucose and oxygen need to get into the cell, and waste substances like carbon dioxide need to get out.

2.

3. a) True b) False c) True d) False e) True

4.

5. By osmosis. The beaker contains a high concentration of water and the celery's cells have a low concentration of water, so some of the water moves into the celery by osmosis and up the celery stalk carrying the red dye with it.

Page 52

1. Photosynthesis is the process by which green plants make food using sunlight.

2. **In any order:**
   a) Light
   b) Carbon dioxide
   c) Water
   d) Chlorophyll

3. **In any order:**
   a) Glucose – some is used immediately by the plant to provide energy via respiration. The rest is converted into insoluble starch which is stored in the leaves, stem or root.
   b) Oxygen – released into the atmosphere as a by-product.

4. Carbon dioxide + Water → Glucose + Oxygen

5. Chlorophyll

6. **In any order: a)** There is less light. **b)** The temperature drops.

Page 53

7. a)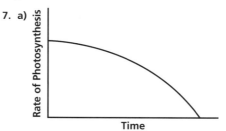

   b) The rate of photosynthesis would gradually decrease as the supply of carbon dioxide in the sealed box was used up by the plant.

8. a) From the soil.
   b) They are absorbed by the plant's roots.
   c) i) To make amino acids which are used to make proteins for growth.
      ii) For chlorophyll production which is required for photosynthesis.

9. The water does not provide the magnesium the shoots need for chlorophyll production (usually obtained from the soil).

Page 54

1. a) The strawberries grown in the greenhouse, where temperature was controlled and maintained at a constant 25°C, gave a higher yield of fruit.
   b) i) and ii) **Accept any suitable answers, e.g.** the plants inside the greenhouse were less vulnerable to insects; the plants inside the greenhouse might have received more/less water than those outside.
   c) i) 50kg
      ii) Light or carbon dioxide could have been acting as a limiting factor.

2. **Accept any suitable answer, e.g.** in a controlled environment optimum conditions can be maintained to achieve maximum yield of fruit.

3. It is easier to control pests and protect the growing plants.

Page 55

1. Producer → Primary Consumer → Secondary Consumer → Tertiary Consumer

2. Light radiation from the Sun.

3. Producers absorb the light from the Sun and convert it into glucose (energy) through photosynthesis.

4. d) ✓

5. Energy is lost through respiration, as heat energy, and in faeces.

6. The mass of living material (dry mass of an organism).

7. Because materials and waste are lost in an organism's faeces.

8. By reducing the number of stages in a food chain, since energy is lost at each stage. Limiting an animal's movement and controlling its temperature reduces the amount of energy lost through heat and movement.

Page 56

1. a)
   - Badger (3rd Consumer)
   - Hedgehog (2nd Consumer)
   - Slug (1st Consumer)
   - Hosta (Producer)

   b)
   - Otter (4th Consumer)
   - Fish (3rd Consumer)
   - Raft Spider (2nd Consumer)
   - Tadpoles (1st Consumer)
   - Green Algae (Producer)

Page 57

1. a) i) So that they do not lose as much energy through heat.
      ii) So that they do not lose as much energy through movement.
   b) **Accept any suitable answer, e.g.** requires less space.
   c) **Accept any suitable answer, e.g.** it is very expensive; more labour intensive.
   d) **Accept any suitable answer, e.g.** it is cruel because it prevents the animal from behaving in a natural way.
   e) **Accept any suitable answer, e.g.** effective ventilation of buildings, to permit air movement and prevent build-up of gases like methane and ammonia.

Page 58

1. **In any order:**
   a) When organisms die and decompose.
   b) When organisms excrete waste.

2. Microorganisms break down the waste and the dead organisms. This decay process releases substances like carbon and nitrogen back into the environment.

3. **Accept any suitable answer, e.g.** in sewage works to break down human waste; in compost heaps to break down material waste.

4. a) 3 b) 4 c) 1 d) 5 e) 2

Page 59

1. a) i) Catalysts ii) Protein iii) Amino acids.
   b) Enzymes are biological catalysts which increase the rate of chemical reactions in an organism. They are protein molecules made up of amino acids.

2. They are folded into a 3-D shape with a site that other molecules can fit into.

3. **In any order:** a) Temperature b) pH levels.

4. a) 37°C
   b) If the body temperature goes much above 37°C, the enzyme's special shape is destroyed (it is denatured).

5. a) and b) **Accept any two from:** respiration; protein synthesis; photosynthesis; digestion.
   Accept any other suitable answers.

6. **Accept any suitable answer, e.g.** to build larger molecules using smaller ones; to enable muscles to contract; to maintain a constant temperature; to make proteins.

Page 60

1. a) The purpose of breathing is to get oxygen from the air into the body, where it can be used for respiration. Respiration takes place in the cells, where oxygen is used to break down glucose molecules to produce energy. Carbon dioxide, the waste product of respiration, is removed from the body by breathing out.
   b) Oxygen
   c) Glucose + Oxygen → Carbon dioxide + Water + Energy
   d) Inside mitochondria.

2. They catalyse the breakdown of large molecules into smaller molecules.

3.
Enzyme	Regions Where It is Found	What It Digests	Molecules Produced
Protease	• Stomach • Pancreas • Small intestine	Proteins	**Amino acids**
Lipase	• **Pancreas** • **Small intestine**	**Lipids**	Fatty acids and glycerols
Amylase	• Salivary glands • Pancreas • Small intestine	**Starch**	Sugars

4. Lipids are fats and oils.

Page 61

1. a) In the liver.
   b) In the gall bladder.
   c) **In any order: i)** It neutralises the acid which was added to food in the stomach, by producing alkaline conditions. **ii)** It emulsifies fats.

2. a) and b) **Accept any suitable answers, e.g.** stomach acid may not be neutralised; fats may be broken down much slower.

3. The enzymes break down stains caused by food and other organic substances.

4. Proteases are used to pre-digest protein in baby food.

5. a) It converts glucose into fructose.
   b) It can be used in smaller amounts than glucose as it is sweeter.

Page 62

1. Enzymes increase the rate of biological chemical reactions.

2. a) They speed up reactions that would normally require high temperatures or high pressures.
   b) It saves energy.

3. a) and b) **Accept any suitable answers, e.g.** in the leather industry to soften hides and remove hair; in the food industry for making the soft centre in sweets.

4. a) At temperatures higher than this the enzymes' shape will be altered and they will stop working.
   b) **Accept any suitable answer, e.g.** some people might be allergic to them.

5. expensive, re-use, soluble, liquids, immobilised, non-reactive

Page 63

1. a) The pancreas.
   b) Insulin.
   c) It converts glucose into insoluble liver glycogen (so it can move out of the blood into the cells), which lowers the concentration of glucose in the blood.

2.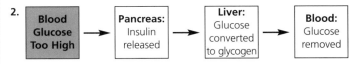
Blood Glucose Too High → Pancreas: Insulin released → Liver: Glucose converted to glycogen → Blood: Glucose removed

3. a) The failure of the pancreas to produce enough insulin, which causes blood glucose levels to rise to very high levels.
   b) **In any order: i)** Diet **ii)** Insulin injections.

Page 64

1. a) The thermoregulatory centre in the brain.
   b) In the skin.

2. a) Cold
   b) Hot
   c) Cold

3. Because the body loses more water than usual through sweating.

4. When blood vessels dilate, this increases heat loss. When blood vessels constrict, this reduces heat loss.

5. **In any order:**
   a) Carbon dioxide: a product of respiration; removed by exhalation.
   b) Urea: a product of the break down of amino acids in the liver; removed by the kidneys (and then through urination via the bladder).

Page 65

1. They removed the pancreases of dogs, and the dogs then developed diabetes.

2. Compounds extracted from the islets of Langerhans (pancreatic cells that produce insulin).

3. The purity (concentration) of the extract they produced.

4. To ensure that the results are reliable.

5. Because humans and dogs are not biologically the same – they could be affected differently.

6. Insulin.

7. a) Just because it worked for one human did not mean that it would work for all.
   b) Modern procedures require drugs to be tested for toxicity before they can be administered to humans. They then need to be tested on a large sample group to collect reliable data about effectiveness and side-effects.

Page 66

1. a) Insulin by injection
   b) An advantage, because it means it has been 'tried and tested'. People know exactly how it works, how reliable it is, etc.

2. **In any order:**
   a) The injection technique.
   b) The site of the injection.
   Accept any other suitable answers.

3. Smoking can cause inconsistent blood glucose levels.

4. **In any order:**
   a) People do not have to inject (easier to administer).
   b) The inhaled doses produced very consistent concentrations of insulin in tests.
   Accept any other suitable answer.

5. Larger doses are required.

6. They may have the potential to cause lung cancer.

7. **Accept any suitable answer, e.g.** young children, the elderly.

Page 67

1. a) ii) ✓ b) iii) ✓ c) i) ✓

2. a) Male b) Female

3.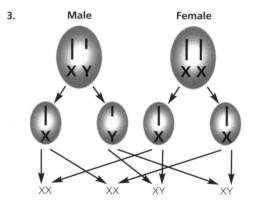

Page 68

1. Mitosis – cell division; involved in asexual reproduction; produces cells with the same number of chromosomes; produces genetically identical clones.
Meiosis – cell division; increases variation in offspring; produces gametes with half the number of chromosomes; involved in sexual reproduction.

2.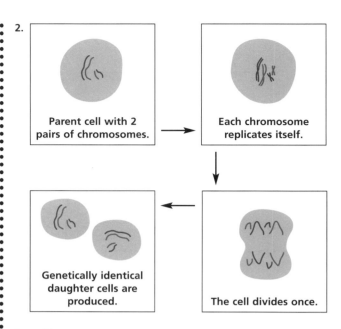

Page 69

1. a) An alternative form of a gene.
   b) The form of the gene that will control the characteristic, even if present on only one chromosome in a pair.
   c) The form of a gene that will control the characteristic only when present on both chromosomes in a pair.

2. a) i) No ii) Yes iii) Yes iv) Yes
   b) i) Brown ii) Brown iii) Blue iv) Brown

3. **In any order:**
   a) HH – tall – homozygous dominant.
   b) Hh – tall – heterozygous.
   c) hh – short – homozygous recessive.

4. a) Heterozygous b) Homozygous dominant
   c) Homozygous recessive d) Heterozygous

Page 70

1. a) i)

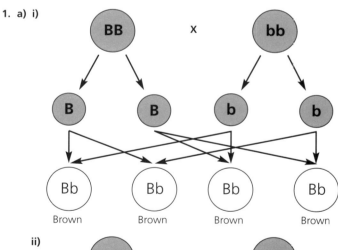

ii)

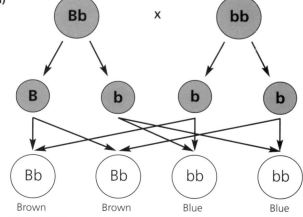

b) i) 0% ii) 50%

2. Each parent may be heterozygous (in which case there is a 25% chance of producing a blue-eyed individual).

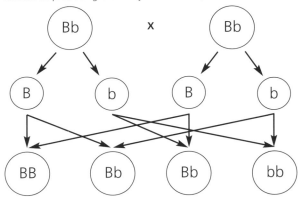

3. c) ✓

Page 71

1. organism, specialised, structure, features, functions, differentiation

2. a) Because they have the potential to be differentiated into different types of cell.
   b) **In any order:** i) Human embryos ii) Human bone marrow.

3. DNA, instructions, amino acids, sequence, cell, organism

4.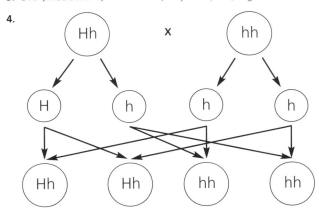

Page 72

1. a) i) Tall ii) Dwarf
   b)
   c)

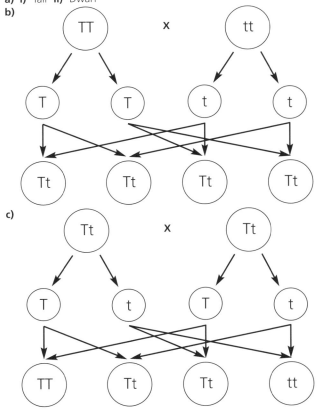

d) To produce reliable results; to ensure that this was something that always happened and that it was not just a coincidence.

Page 73

1. a) Because if allowed to develop naturally, they would grow into a baby.
   b) The embryos from which the stem cells are taken are grown in labs and are only a few days old. Therefore, they are only tiny balls of cells.
   c) Those that believe that embryos should be treated as people.

2. a) A positive effect – they will suffer less and live longer.
   b) The population size will increase because people will live for longer.
   c) **i) and ii) Accept any sensible answers, e.g.** there will be more people competing for jobs / resources like food / housing.

3. a) Eggs and sperm are taken from the parents. The eggs are then fertilised and develop into embryos in the laboratory.
   b) Because the embryos are created from the woman's egg and the man's semen and could, if allowed, potentially develop into a child.

Page 74

1. a) i) For
      ii) Against
      iii) Against
      iv) For
      v) Against
      vi) For
   b) The money that is currently spent treating these diseases could be put to use elsewhere.
      Accept any other sensible answer.
   c) Disease is a natural way of controlling the population.
      Accept any other sensible answer.
   d) An embryo is a new life, destroying it is murder.
      Accept any other sensible answer.

2. a) **Accept any sensible answer, e.g.** it could lead to the creation of the 'perfect' race; it is unnatural, and therefore morally wrong.
   b) It may reduce variation – some characteristics may be lost permanently (e.g. brown eyes if everybody pre-selected blue eyes for their children).

Page 75

1. a)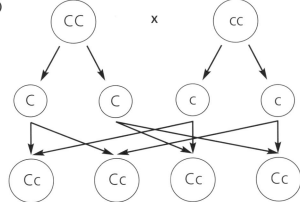

   b) 100%
   c) Both parents could be heterozygous carriers, in which case there would be 25% chance of producing a child with cystic fibrosis.

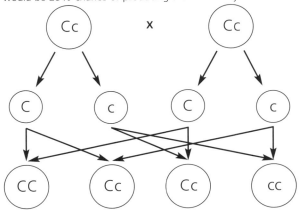

Page 76

1. **a)** Enzyme **b)** Tissue **c)** Organ **d)** Vacuole **e)** Cell **f)** Gamete
   g) Catalyst **h)** Insoluble **i)** Urea **j)** Permeable **k)** Allele **l)** Lipase
   m) Amylase **n)** Protease **o)** Specialised **p)** Decay **q)** Anaerobic
   r) Aerobic **s)** Soluble **t)** Diffusion **u)** Osmosis **v)** Mitosis
   w) Meiosis **x)** Fertilisation **y)** Bile **z)** Core **aa)** Thermoregulation
   bb) Biomass **cc)** pH **dd)** Capillary **ee)** Ribosomes **ff)** Chloroplast
   gg) Chlorophyll **hh)** Photosynthesis **ii)** Marrow **jj)** DNA
   kk) Cytoplasm **ll)** Urine **mm)** Microorganisms

Page 77

2. [Completed wordsearch grid]

Page 78

1. **a)** ii) requires energy from respiration
   b) i) against the concentration gradient
   c) ii) are not examples of active transport

2. **a)** In any order:
      i) Breathing system.
      ii) Digestive system.
   b) In any order:
      i) Large surface area – villi in the small intestine and alveoli in the lungs provide a large surface area for the efficient exchange of materials.
      ii) Good blood supply – for transporting substances to and from the site of exchange.

3. **a)** Carbon dioxide diffuses from the blood into the alveoli. Oxygen diffuses from the alveoli into the blood.
   b) No diffusion, because the oxygen and carbon dioxide are moving along concentration gradients (not against them).

Page 79

1. Transpiration.

2. **a)** i) Water vapour from the leaf cells evaporates through the stomata, which open to allow carbon dioxide in for photosynthesis.
      ii) It had no water. Lack of water makes the plant cells flaccid.

3. **a)** Close the stomata.
   b) Photosynthesis.
   c) Because the stomata close to reduce water loss. The stomata need to be open for carbon dioxide to be taken in for photosynthesis.
   d) Guard cells.

4. The leaves of broad-leaved plants require water and light. There is less water and light available in winter so, if the plant loses its leaves, it only needs enough water to keep its stem alive.

Page 80

1. In any order:
   a) A large surface area.
   b) A method of transporting the substances to and from the exchange site.

2. **Accept any suitable answer.**

Page 81

1. **a)** It carries blood from the heart to all the body's cells to supply them with food and oxygen, and carries waste products away from the cells.
   b) i) Artery ii) Vein iii) Capillaries iv) Vein v) Artery
   c) and d)

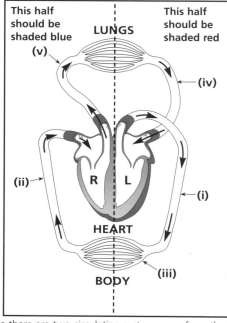

   e) Because there are two circulation systems: one from the heart to the lungs and back to the heart, the other from the heart to all the other organs and back again.

2. Red blood cells (haemoglobin).

3. **a)** Less oxygen is available, so they need more red blood cells to get the required amounts to their cells.
   b) It leads to an increase in red blood cells, so they can get more oxygen to their cells for respiration during the race.

4. In any order:
   a) It transports carbon dioxide from the organs to the lungs.
   b) It transports glucose from the small intestine to the organs.
   c) It transports waste from the liver to the kidneys.

Page 82

1. The purpose of breathing is to get oxygen from the air into the body, where it can be used for respiration. Respiration takes place in the cells, where oxygen is used to break down glucose molecules to produce energy. Carbon dioxide, the waste product of respiration, is removed from the body by breathing out.

2. **a)** Oxygen.
   b) Glucose.
   c) To provide energy.
   d) Carbon dioxide and water.
   e) Glucose + Oxygen → Carbon dioxide + Water + Energy

3. **a)** Anaerobic respiration.
   b) Glucose → Energy + Lactic acid
   c) Lactic acid has accumulated in her muscle tissues. The muscles can no longer contract efficiently and start to feel weak and rubbery.

Page 83

4. **a)** iii) ✓
   b) Because aerobic respiration involves the complete breakdown of glucose. Anaerobic respiration involves the incomplete breakdown of glucose.
   c) It produces energy much more quickly than aerobic respiration.

5. a) They were respiring aerobically.
   b) They were respiring anaerobically, so their bodies need to obtain as much oxygen as possible to break down the lactic acid and repay the oxygen debt.

6. The extra oxygen needed to counteract the harmful effects of anaerobic respiration (i.e. break down the lactic acid that has accumulated) is called an oxygen debt. The oxygen debt needs to be repaid after exercise: this is done through deep breathing.

Page 84

1. a) It increases.
   b) It will increase (and become deeper).
   c) The body is trying to obtain plenty of oxygen, and pump it quickly round the body to the cells, for respiration (to provide energy).

2. a) Because the glucose in the blood is broken down to provide energy.
   b) There may not be sufficient glucose in the blood to be broken down to provide the energy needed to perform at her most efficient level.
   c) So that their bodies have plenty of glucose which can be broken down to produce energy.

Page 85

1. a) **In any order:**
      i) Blood vessels.
      ii) Tubules.
   b) The ureter.
   c) The bladder.
   d) None.
   e) i) Water, ions and urea.
      ii) Excretion.
   f) i) Selective reabsorption.
      ii) Active transport.
      iii) Respiration.

2. She is dehydrated, so there is less water to be removed. This means that the urine is less diluted. She could have prevented this by drinking more water before and during her bike ride.

Page 86

1. When the kidneys fail.

2. a) The person's blood flows through the machine, where it is separated from the dialysis fluid by a partially permeable membrane. The membrane allows all the urea and any excess substances to pass from the blood into the dialysis fluid.
   b) To ensure that useful substances like glucose and essential mineral ions are not lost through diffusion.

3. To replace a failed/diseased kidney with a new healthy one if both kidneys have stopped working.

4. a) To minimise the risk of rejection by the recipient's immune system.
   b) If the donor is a close relative.
   c) **In any order:**
      i) The recipient's bone marrow must be irradiated to stop production of white blood cells.
      ii) The recipient is treated with drugs which suppress the immune system.
      iii) The recipient is kept in sterile conditions for a period after the operation.

Page 87

1. a) i) and ii) **Accept any two from:** bacterial infection; high blood pressure; external injury.
   b) **In any order:**
      i) Failure to pass water.
      ii) Build up of sodium ions and urea in the blood.
      iii) Blood protein in urine.

2. a) **In any order:**
      i) No risk of rejection.
      ii) Readily available.
   b) **In any order:**
      i) Regular sessions take up a lot of time.
      ii) The diet has to be strictly regulated.
   Accept any other sensible answers.

3. a) **In any order:**
      i) No need for regular dialysis sessions.
      ii) The success rate is high.
      iii) A healthy person can donate a kidney and live perfectly well with one kidney.
   b) **In any order:**
      i) A donated kidney must be transplanted within 12 hours.
      ii) Risk of rejection.
      iii) Patient may need to take anti-rejection drugs for life.
   Accept any other sensible answers.

4. Yes, because it is possible for a person to live perfectly healthily with just one fully functioning kidney.

Page 88

1. Yeast is a single-celled organism with a nucleus, cytoplasm, vacuole and membrane surrounded by a cell wall.

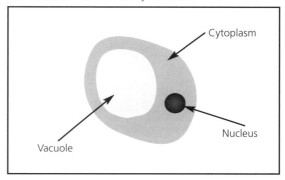

2. a) Glucose → Ethanol + Carbon dioxide + Energy
   b) Fermentation

3. Glucose + Oxygen → Water + Carbon dioxide + Energy

4. The active yeast respires carbon dioxide which makes the dough rise. The bubbles of gas expand when the bread is baked.

5. Yeast is added to a solution of broken down starch and fermentation then takes place. Carbon dioxide bubbles off to leave alcohol.

Page 89

1. a) Microorganisms did not appear on meat broth that had been sealed tightly in jars and boiled for 30 minutes.
   b) Because no microorganisms appeared on the meat broth which was tightly sealed up, this meant that life did not spontaneously originate from unliving matter.

2. All living things come from cells and new cells come from existing cells.

3. a) A nutrient solution was poured into a flask. The neck of the flask was melted and bent over. The solution in the flask was boiled to kill microorganisms and remove air, then the solution was left in the flask for a few weeks, without decaying. The same was done to a nutrient solution in a flask which had the neck snapped off. This flask solution decayed within days.
   b) It proved that microorganisms were found in the air and that living things come from other living things.

Page 90

1. fermenters, oxygen, stirrer, temperature, heat, temperature/pH, temperature/pH.

2. a) Penicillin.
   b) Sugar and other nutrients.

3. a) Mycoprotein.
   b) Starch.

4. a) Anaerobic respiration.
   b) By carrying out the process in a closed system, which keeps all oxygen out.

5. a) Sugar cane juices or glucose from maize starch.
   b) To power motor vehicles.
   Accept any other suitable answers.

Page 91

1. a) Fossil fuels are non-renewable resources – they cannot be replaced in a lifetime.
   b) Fossil fuels release carbon dioxide (a greenhouse gas) and pollutants when they are burned.

2. a) **In any order:**
   i) It is a renewable energy supply.
   ii) It is cleaner than fossil fuels.
   iii) It is a cheap energy source.
   Accept any other suitable answers.
   b) **Accept any suitable answers.**
   c) and d) **In any order:**
   i) It can take one month to produce biogas – Economy.
   ii) The initial start-up is expensive – Economy.
   iii) Storage facilities are needed – Environment.
   Accept any other suitable answers.

3. **Accept any suitable answer, e.g.** German farmers using manure to produce biogas to heat their own homes.

Page 92

1. a) A batch biogas generator.
   b) A continuous biogas generator.
   c) i) and ii) **Accept any two from:** It takes time and energy to set up; Only small amounts are produced; Process can take up to 4 weeks.
   Accept any other suitable answers.
   d) i) and ii) **Accept any two from:** It is more expensive to set up than a batch generator; It cannot control temperature; Needs a continuous feed of waste; Large amounts of gas need storing.
   Accept any other suitable answers.
   e) The continuous biogas generator. Although it is expensive to set up, once it is running it is very efficient. It can continue for long periods of time without a break and does not need to be cleaned like the batch generator.

Page 93

1. a) Agar.
   b) i) Proteins.
   ii) Mineral ions.
   iii) Carbohydrates.
   iv) Vitamins.

2. a) A pressure cooker which sterilises Petri dishes and the agar by exposing them to high temperatures and high pressure.
   b) A loop made out of (nichrome) wire inserted into a wooden handle. It is used to transfer microorganisms to the culture medium.
   c) i) The autoclave is used to sterilise the Petri dishes and the culture medium by killing off unwanted microorganisms using high temperatures and high pressure.
   ii) The inoculating loop is heated to red heat in a Bunsen flame to sterilise it. After cooling for five seconds, it is used to transfer microorganisms to the culture medium.
   iii) Once the agar has been poured into the Petri dish and has cooled, the dish is sealed and stored upside down so that condensation forms in the lid and no microorganisms can get in.
   d) They would affect the results of the investigation and may produce undesirable substances which could be harmful.

3. To prevent the growth of pathogens that can be harmful to humans.

Page 94

1. Crossword solution:
   - 1 Across: OXYGENDEBT
   - 3 Down: BI...
   - 4 Across: PLASMA
   - 5 Down: MT
   - 6 Down: ANAEROBIC
   - 7 Across: OSMOSIS
   - 8 Across: ACTIVETRANSPORT
   - 9 Down: GD
   - 10 Across: TRANSPIRATION
   - 11 Down: LV
   - 12 Down: PES
   - 13 Across: VILLI
   - 14 Down: IA
   - 15 Down: S
   - 16 Across: WILT
   - 17 Across: INCUBATE
   - 18 Down: D
   - 19 Down: RE
   - 20 Across: MALT
   - 21 Across: DIALYSIS
   - 22 Across: MEDIUM
   - 23 Across: UREA

Page 95

1. a) iii) ✓
   b) ii) ✓
   c) i) ✓
   d) iii) ✓
   e) i) ✓
   f) ii) ✓
   g) iii) ✓

AQA GCSE Science

An invaluable revision guide carefully matched to AQA GCSE Science (Specifications A and B), providing full coverage of the core content on the programme of study for KS4 science. Plus, supporting workbook.

Cat No: 460

Cat No: 461

Whichever additional options you choose, our complete range of guides and student workbooks for AQA GCSE science will meet your revision needs.

Cat No: 462

Cat No: 463

Cat No: 464

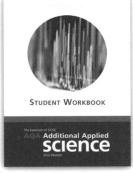
Cat No: 465

Cat No: 482

Cat No: 481

Cat No: 480

Cat No: 485

Cat No: 484

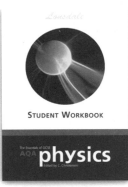
Cat No: 483

This answer book should be used to mark pupils' responses to the questions in *The Essentials of GCSE AQA Biology Student Workbook*.

Westmorland House, Elmsfield Park, Holme, Carnforth, Lancashire LA6 1RJ
Telephone - Sales: **015395 65920** General Enquiries: **015395 65921** Accounts: **015395 65922**
Fax: **015395 64167** email: **orders@lonsdalesrg.co.uk** web: **www.lonsdalesrg.co.uk**

ISBN 1-905129-86-6

Published by Lonsdale A Division of Huveaux Plc

How Science Works

To answer the questions on this page, you will have to recall scientific facts and draw upon your knowledge of how science works, e.g. scientific procedures, issues and ideas.

1 Name two harmful substances that cannabis contains in higher amounts than tobacco.

   a) ....   b) ....

2 Choose one of your answers to Question 1, and describe what potential health problems the substance can cause.

   ....

3 Name two other health problems that have been linked to cannabis use.

   a) ....   b) ....

4 Many people who smoke cannabis mix it with tobacco. What additional problems could this cause?

   ....

5 Cannabis has been found to provide relief from the symptoms of some diseases. Name two of these diseases.

   a) ....   b) ....

6 a) Cannabis is sometimes described as a 'gateway' drug. What does that mean?

   ....

   ....

   b) Why do some people dispute that cannabis is a 'gateway' drug?

   ....

   ....

7 In January 2004, cannabis was reclassified from a Class B to a Class C drug in the UK. Some people believe that cannabis use will increase as a result of this, and that this will also lead to an increase in the use of other illegal drugs. In your own words, explain why they might think this.

   ....

   ....

   ....

How Science Works

To answer the questions on this page, you will have to recall scientific facts and draw upon your knowledge of how science works, e.g. scientific procedures, issues and ideas.

1 During the 1940s and 1950s the number of fatalities caused by lung cancer increased.

a) Name two factors that scientists first suggested as possible causes for this.

i) ....

ii) ....

b) Which professional body commissioned an investigation into the link between tobacco and lung cancer?

....

c) In your own words, explain the findings of this investigation.

....

....

....

2 Complete the timeline, to show how the link between smoking tobacco and lung cancer was gradually accepted, by using the appropriate letter to indicate when each key event took place.

a)	The government in the UK accepts that there is a strong link between smoking tobacco and lung cancer.
b)	Tobacco companies are forced to pay compensation to individuals suffering from tobacco-related illnesses.
c)	Smoking in public places becomes illegal in Scotland.
d)	There is a rise in the number of deaths caused by lung cancer.
e)	The media bring the link to public attention.
f)	The Medical Research Council publishes a report proposing a link between smoking tobacco and lung cancer, but it is widely ignored.
g)	The fact that smokers are at greater risk from lung cancer is widely accepted. The number of smokers in England has fallen by 50% since 1950.
h)	Smoking in enclosed public places is outlawed in England.

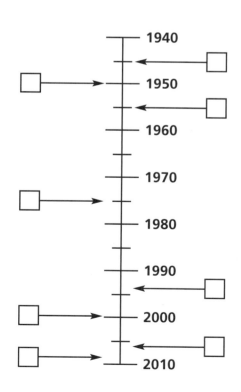

26 BIOLOGY WORKBOOK – Revision Guide Reference: Page 26 © Letts and Lonsdale

How Science Works

To answer the questions on this page, you will have to recall scientific facts and draw upon your knowledge of how science works, e.g. scientific procedures, issues and ideas.

1 Explain briefly why a heavy smoker might find it very difficult to give up smoking.

....

....

....

2 Below are four methods that can be used when trying to give up smoking. Use an arrow to link each one to the correct explanation.

a) Nicotine replacement products, e.g. gum, patches and lozenges.

This helps you deal with the emotional and psychological aspects of quitting smoking.

b) Hypnotherapy

This helps relieve the withdrawal symptoms and cravings, helping you to break the psychological habit.

c) Acupuncture

This relies entirely on willpower to stop.

d) Cold turkey

This stimulates pressure points on the body and helps to alleviate withdrawal symptoms.

3 Read the following information about Zyban carefully.

Zyban is a relatively new drug. It is an anti-depressant that can be used to help people give up smoking. It is suitable for heavy smokers, who are motivated to quit, and is only available by prescription from a doctor.

Zyban has been shown to alleviate many of the withdrawal symptoms associated with quitting smoking, including cravings, anxiety, irritability, lack of concentration and depression. It is not suitable for people with a history of fits or eating disorders and should not be used during pregnancy. Possible side effects include insomnia, dry mouth and headaches.

a) List three potential benefits of taking Zyban.

i) ....

ii) ....

iii) ....

b) List three potential problems of taking Zyban.

i) ....

ii) ....

iii) ....

Unit 1 – 11.4

Bacteria and Viruses

1 What is a pathogen?

_____

2 Name two illnesses caused by bacteria.

a) _____ b) _____

3 Name two illnesses caused by viruses.

a) _____ b) _____

Defence Against Pathogens

4 Describe two ways in which white blood cells fight pathogens that invade the body.

a) _____

b) _____

Treatment of Disease

5 Fill in the missing words to complete the following passage.

The symptoms of a disease can often be alleviated using _____. However, these drugs do not _____ pathogens. Antibiotics can be used to kill infective _____. But they cannot kill _____, which live and _____ inside the body's cells.

Overuse of Antibiotics

6 Number these statements from **1** to **5** to show the sequence of events that can lead to the development of superbugs like MRSA, which are highly resistant to antibiotics.

a) Antibiotics kill most of the bacteria, but the resistant individuals survive. ☐

d) In a population of bacteria, some individuals will have a natural resistance to antibiotics. ☐

b) Eventually only the resistant form exists. ☐

e) The number of resistant individuals in a population increases. ☐

c) These bacteria reproduce. ☐

How Science Works

To answer the questions on this page, you will have to recall scientific facts and draw upon your knowledge of how science works, e.g. scientific procedures, issues and ideas.

1 Semmelweiss realised that the spread of infections could be reduced if doctors washed their hands between dealing with different patients. Explain how this works.

....

....

2 In what century did Semmelweiss make this discovery? ....

3 Hygiene is a top priority in modern hospitals. In the space below, design a poster to be displayed in hospital wards. Include five relevant practices that the nurses should carry out to help stop the spread of infection.

How Science Works

To answer the questions on this page, you will have to recall scientific facts and draw upon your knowledge of how science works, e.g. scientific procedures, issues and ideas.

1) In the 19th century, the average Briton could only expect to live into their 50s, and many didn't even make it to adulthood. One of the reasons for this was disease. Diseases like measles, mumps, tuberculosis (TB), syphilis and cholera were rife, and nearly always fatal. TB was responsible for approximately 25% of all deaths in Europe at that time!

a) Use the Internet, library or another secondary source to find out whether each of the diseases listed in the table is caused by a bacteria or virus.

Disease	Cause
i) Measles	
ii) Mumps	
iii) Tuberculosis	
iv) Syphilis	
v) Cholera	

b) Tuberculosis, syphilis and cholera are far less common in modern Britain, and although these conditions are serious they are often treatable.

In terms of medical practices, explain the reason for this turnaround.

....

....

....

c) In terms of pathogens, why do you think measles and mumps are more common in modern Britain than TB, syphilis and cholera?

....

2) There has been a lot of media coverage relating to bird influenza recently.

a) What type of microorganism causes influenza? ....

b) Although bird flu normally only affects birds, why are scientists concerned that an epidemic could break out in the human population?

....

....

How Science Works

To answer the questions on this page, you will have to recall scientific facts and draw upon your knowledge of how science works, e.g. scientific procedures, issues and ideas.

1 Read this information carefully before answering the questions below:

Vaccine:	Revaxis
Main Use:	Booster vaccination against diphtheria, tetanus and polio
Recommended For:	All school leavers (between 13 and 18 years of age)
Availability:	Available to all UK residents free of charge

Notes: To prevent adverse effects, this vaccination should not be given to people who have been vaccinated against diphtheria or tetanus within the last five years.

Some of the possible known side effects of the vaccination are nausea and vomiting, fever, vertigo (an inner-ear problem that affects balance), headaches, swollen glands and pain in the muscle or joints.

a) Diphtheria, Tetanus and Polio can all be fatal. Use the Internet, a library or another secondary source to find out what part of the body each disease affects and what some of the symptoms are. Record your findings in the table below. Give three examples of symptoms for each disease.

Disease	Part of Body Affected	Symptoms
i) Diphtheria		• • •
ii) Tetanus		• • •
iii) Polio		• • •

b) List two advantages of the Revaxis vaccine.

i) ....

ii) ....

c) List two disadvantages of the Revaxis vaccine.

i) ....

ii) ....

Unit 1 – 11.5

Competition and Adaptation

1 For each word given below, place a tick beside the correct definition.

a) **Population**

   i) The total number of organisms living in a particular habitat. ☐

   ii) The total number of individuals of the same species living in a particular habitat. ☐

   iii) The total number of animals living in a particular habitat. ☐

b) **Community**

   i) All the organisms that coexist in a particular habitat. ☐

   ii) A small group of organisms that are dependant on each other for survival. ☐

   iii) All the natural resources that support the organisms in a particular habitat. ☐

c) **Adaptation**

   i) A significant change in the size of a population. ☐

   ii) The process by which the different organisms in a habitat learn to share resources. ☐

   iii) The development of a feature, which helps an organism to compete and survive in a particular environment. ☐

2 Unscramble the letters below to find four factors that can affect the size of a population.

a) ASSEEID ....

b) RATIOMING ....

c) DATEPRION ....

d) CONOTEIMPIT ....

3 Name the three main resources that the different organisms in a habitat compete for.

a) .... b) .... c) ....

4 Polar bears are found throughout the Arctic. They spend most of their time on ice floes, and tend to stay close to the water when on the mainland. Seals form the basis of their diet. Name three adaptations that help polar bears to survive in the icy wilderness of the Arctic.

a) ....

b) ....

c) ....

How Science Works

To answer the questions on this page, you will have to recall scientific facts and draw upon your knowledge of how science works, e.g. scientific procedures, issues and ideas.

1 Read these descriptions of real adaptations that have occurred in different species over long periods of time. From the options below, choose which environment you think each species can be found in, based on the adaptation. Write your answer alongside in the space provided.

    Cave   Desert   Mangrove Swamp (fills with sea water at high tide)

    Rainforest   Mountain   Depths of Ocean

a) This animal's eyes have disappeared but the number of sensory receptors in other parts of its body has increased. _____

b) These trees have developed a tolerance to salt and their roots protrude above water. _____

c) This mammal has developed a prehensile tail, which can grasp hold of things. _____

d) These plants have no leaves, which reduces transpiration and conserves water. _____

e) This organism can survive in pressures high enough to crush other species. _____

f) These animals have developed large lungs, and blood cells that can cope with low levels of oxygen. _____

2 Penguins have webbed feet and streamlined bodies. They have thick skin, with a thick layer of fat, and instinctively huddle together. Suggest how these adaptations might help a penguin survive in its natural habitat.

_____

_____

3 Below are three adaptations that lions have developed. For each one, suggest how it might help them to compete and survive.

a) Lions have loose skin around their bellies because…

_____

b) Lions have large forepaws with long, retractable claws because…

_____

c) Lions are a golden colour because…

_____

How Science Works

To answer the questions on this page, you will have to recall scientific facts and draw upon your knowledge of how science works, e.g. scientific procedures, issues and ideas.

1 What three factors do organisms compete for?

a) _____ b) _____ c) _____

2 A class compiled a list of organisms that could be found in the small wood at the bottom of their school playing field:

Oak Tree; Grey Squirrel; Fox; Fern; Centipede; Ground Beetle; Caterpillar; Shrew; Robin; Bluebell; Chaffinch; Green Woodpecker; Beech Tree; Woodlouse.

The bluebells have to compete with ferns for space on the woodland floor, water and nutrients in the soil, and light for photosynthesis.

For each species given below, write the name of one other species they are likely to be in competition with and explain your answer.

a) Oak Tree Competitor: _____

Why: _____

b) Centipede Competitor: _____

Why: _____

c) Robin Competitor: _____

Why: _____

d) In some areas of the wood, the leaf canopy of the trees is very dense and hardly any light reaches the woodland floor. Explain how this is likely to affect the distribution of the plants and insects.

Unit 1 – 11.6

Genetic Information

1 Use the following words to label the diagram alongside.

   a) Chromosomes

   b) Cell

   c) Nucleus

2 Below are three definitions. Write the word being described alongside each one.

   a) The name given to the sex cells in organisms that produce offspring by sexual reproduction.

   b) These are found in the nucleus of cells and occur in pairs, except for in the sex cells.

   c) These appear on the structures described in part **b)** and control the development of different characteristics in an organism.

Causes of Variation

3 a) What is variation?

   b) Name the two causes of variation and provide an example for each one.

      i) Cause: _____ Example: _____

      ii) Cause: _____ Example: _____

Effect of Reproduction on Variation

4 In your own words, explain why variation occurs in offspring produced by sexual reproduction, but is rare in offspring produced by asexual reproduction.

Unit 1 – 11.6

Reproducing Plants Artificially

1 Number each of these statements from **1** to **6** to show the sequence in which new plants can be cloned from an existing plant by taking cuttings.

a) This is inserted into a mixture of sand and peat moss and watered thoroughly. ☐

b) A plant shows a desirable characteristic. ☐

c) The young plant will grow and develop showing the same characteristics as the parent. ☐

d) Roots will start to develop after a few weeks if a damp atmosphere is maintained. ☐

e) The gardener transfers the cutting into a pot containing soil and fertiliser. ☐

f) The gardener removes a section of stem 4–6 inches long. ☐

Cloning

2 This flow chart shows the sequence of events used to clone sheep by embryo transplantation. Write a brief description of what is happening at each stage of the process.

Stage 1:

Stage 2:

Stage 3:

Stage 4:

Unit 1 – 11.6

Reasons for Genetic Modification

1 Fill in the missing words to complete the following passage about genetic modification.

Genetic modification is a process in which genetic information from one _____ is transferred into another. The genes are often transferred at an _____ stage of development, so that the organism will develop with the desired _____. More organisms with the same characteristics can be produced if the genetically modified organism is then _____.

2 Name two ways in which tomatoes have been genetically modified to make them more appealing to consumers.

a) _____

b) _____

Genetic Engineering

3 Complete the crossword below.

Across
1. These structures carry an organism's genetic information (11)
5. A ring of bacterial DNA capable of multiplying (7)
7. A disease caused when the body cannot produce enough 6 Down naturally (8)
8. This appears on 1 Across and controls the development of a particular characteristic (4)

Down
1. The building blocks of all organisms, these hold genetic information in their nuclei (5)
2. Another word used to describe the way in which single celled organisms multiply (9)
3. These are used to remove precise sections of 1 Across for genetic engineering (7)
4. This organ produces the hormone needed to control blood sugar levels (8)
6. The hormone that controls blood sugar levels, which can be produced by genetic engineering (7).
7. 1 Across are made from these molecules, which are shaped in a double helix (3)

How Science Works

To answer the questions on this page, you will have to recall scientific facts and draw upon your knowledge of how science works, e.g. scientific procedures, issues and ideas.

1. An economic issue is usually concerned with money: how much is available, how it is best spent and how more can be made.

Suggest one economic argument relating to the production of GM crops. Indicate whether it is an argument **for** or **against** by putting a line through one of the options.

An Economic Argument For / Against GM crops:

....
....

2. A social issue is one that affects the population of a community, town or country as a whole.

Name one social argument concerning the production of GM crops. Indicate whether it is an argument for or against by putting a line through one of the options.

A Social Argument For / Against GM crops:

....
....

3. An ethical issue is one concerned with what is morally right and wrong. For example, most people believe it is wrong (unethical) to deceive, or lie to, someone else.

Suggest one ethical argument concerning the production of GM crops. Indicate whether it is an argument for or against by putting a line through one of the options.

An Ethical Argument For / Against GM crops:

....
....

4. Suggest one economic argument concerning cloning animals. Indicate whether it is an argument for or against by putting a line through one of the options.

An Economic Argument For / Against Cloning Animals:

....

Unit 1 – 11.7

Theory of Evolution

1) Which of these passages best describes the theory of evolution? Use a tick to indicate your choice.

a) Most species have been around since the Earth was first formed although they have had to change a bit to adapt to changes in their environment. ☐

b) Animals developed from insects, and insects developed from plants. ☐

c) All species in existence, and those that are now extinct, developed from simple life forms over a period of approximately 3 billion years. ☐

The Reasons for Extinction of Species

2) In your own words, explain how the following factors could lead to the extinction of species.

a) Competition

b) Environmental Change

The Fossil Record

3) What evidence do fossils provide for evolution? Explain your answer.

Evolution by Natural Selection

4) Which individuals in a population are most likely to survive and breed successfully?

5) Is each generation likely to be better adapted or less well adapted to their environment than the previous one?

6) What other event can lead to a change in a species?

How Science Works

To answer the questions on this page, you will have to recall scientific facts and draw upon your knowledge of how science works, e.g. scientific procedures, issues and ideas.

1 a) With regards to the origins of life, what do the Creationist Theory and Intelligent Design Theory have in common?

b) Explain briefly what the main difference is between these theories and Darwin's theory.

2 Darwin and Lamarck both believed that characteristics could be passed on from one generation to the next. What is the main difference between their theories?

3 In the early 1800s, religion had a strong influence in society. How is that likely to have affected the way in which people responded to Darwin's theory of evolution?

4 Suggest one other reason why Darwin's theory of evolution was only gradually accepted.

5 The fossil record is often cited as evidence for Darwin's theory of evolution.

a) How does it support his theory?

b) Creationists do not believe that the fossil record provides evidence for Darwin's theory. Suggest one reason why.

How Science Works

To answer the questions on this page, you will have to recall scientific facts and draw upon your knowledge of how science works, e.g. scientific procedures, issues and ideas.

1) The diagram alongside shows fossils in a cross-section of rock.

a) Label the youngest layer of rock and the oldest layer of rock.

b) Explain briefly, how a fossil record like this could provide evidence of evolution.

2) Think about the rock cycle. Rocks can move around; some get pushed upwards and others get forced downwards and melt into magma, and rock on the surface is slowly eroded.

Explain what effect this will have on the fossil record.

3) A fossil is created because an animal or plant dies and falls into silt or mud, so it is broken down very slowly. However, most organisms decay fairly quickly.

Explain what effect this will have on the fossil record.

4) Most fossils are made from the hard parts of animals, e.g. teeth, bones and shells.

Explain what effect this will have on the fossil record (hint: think about animals with tentacles and boneless protrusions).

Unit 1 – 11.8

The Population Explosion

1) At the moment, the human population is increasing exponentially.

a) What does this mean?

b) Sketch a graph which illustrates exponential increase in the space provided.

c) Suggest two reasons for this population 'explosion'.

   i)

   ii)

d) As a result, natural resources like coal and oil are being used up quickly. Why is this a problem?

e) Identify two other environmental problems caused by the rapidly growing human population.

   i)

   ii)

Pollution

2) This wordsearch contains 8 pollutants produced by man-made activity. Circle each one on the grid and add it to the list alongside.

C	A	B	B	N	A	G	E	E	A	T	I	E
I	S	H	R	I	E	A	L	L	Y	Y	D	D
U	P	E	S	T	I	C	I	D	E	I	M	I
S	M	R	Y	R	I	T	M	A	X	K	E	X
M	S	B	M	O	Y	M	O	O	U	T	H	O
O	W	I	A	G	T	E	I	R	A	N	D	I
K	I	C	L	E	I	D	K	E	E	B	R	D
E	U	I	S	N	N	S	E	G	L	S	P	R
R	O	D	U	O	T	S	Y	A	O	U	M	U
I	G	E	B	X	H	T	T	W	H	I	N	F
F	E	R	T	I	L	I	S	E	R	K	T	L
H	A	A	T	D	I	A	M	S	M	A	D	U
C	B	U	T	E	I	X	Y	D	O	N	Z	S

i)

ii)

iii)

iv)

v)

vi)

vii)

viii)

Unit 1 – 11.8

Deforestation

1 What is deforestation?

2 Give two reasons why deforestation is taking place.

a)

b)

3 Some conservationists estimate that if deforestation continues at the current rate, the world's rainforests could vanish within 100 years. Give three reasons why this is a problem.

a)

b)

c)

Sustainable Development

4 Summarise the aims of sustainable development in a single sentence.

The Greenhouse Effect

5 Name two greenhouse gases.

a)   b)

6 In your own words, explain how these gases are causing the overall temperature of the planet to gradually rise.

Unit 1 – 11.8

Sustainable Development (cont.)

1 Name the three key related issues that sustainable development is concerned with.

a) _____

b) _____

c) _____

2 Which definition best describes a sustainable resource? Use a tick to indicate your choice.

A sustainable resource is a resource that…

a) is only available in limited supplies and will eventually run out. ☐

b) is available in limitless quantities. ☐

c) can be maintained in sufficient quantities if managed carefully. ☐

3 Name two ways in which sustainable resources can be maintained.

a) _____

b) _____

4 Choose one of your answers from Question 3 and provide an example of how this has been put into practice.

_____

_____

_____

Endangered Species

5 a) How has the previous neglect of sustainable development led to the osprey becoming an endangered species?

_____

_____

b) What action has been taken to prevent it from becoming extinct?

_____

How Science Works

To answer the questions on this page, you will have to recall scientific facts and draw upon your knowledge of how science works, e.g. scientific procedures, issues and ideas.

1) One way in which scientists can monitor global warming is to measure the size of mountain glaciers (large rivers of ice).

If the overall temperature of the planet is rising, what effect would you expect this to have on the glaciers?

2) Scientists measured the volume of a glacier in cubic kilometres, km^3 (Measurement 1). They measured the volume of the same glacier again 10 years later (Measurement 2), and performed the following calculation:

Measurement 2 (km^3) - Measurement 1 (km^3)

a) What would the answer to this calculation tell them?

b) What would it mean if the answer was a positive number?

c) What would it mean if the answer was a negative number?

This table shows their results:

Time (Years)	Change in Volume (km^3)	Cumulative Change in Volume
10	-1000	-1000
20	-1000	-2000
30	-1250	-3250
40	-2000	-5250

d) What does this data show?

How Science Works

To answer the questions on this page, you will have to recall scientific facts and draw upon your knowledge of how science works, e.g. scientific procedures, issues and ideas.

1 Carbon monoxide is a pollutant gas, which is the product of incomplete combustion. This means it is found in the exhaust emissions of motor vehicles.

The village of Loxley has a busy road running through it, but a new bypass is due to open soon. The local residents think that this will reduce carbon monoxide levels in the village centre. To test this, they decide to measure carbon monoxide levels in the village centre before and after the bypass is opened.

a) Name two things the local residents can do to ensure that this is a fair test.

i) ....

ii) ....

b) Here are the results collected:

Measurement	1	2	3	4	5
Before Bypass Opens	4.5	4.3	4.4	4.4	4.5
After Bypass Opens	0.8	0.7	0.8	2.3	0.6

i) Why do you think each measurement was repeated several times?

....

....

ii) Suggest one reason why the measurements in each set might vary.

....

iii) The fourth measurement taken after the bypass opened is much higher than the other measurements in that set. What does that suggest?

....

iv) What conclusions can be drawn from this data?

....

....

....

How Science Works

To answer the questions on this page, you will have to recall scientific facts and draw upon your knowledge of how science works, e.g. scientific procedures, issues and ideas.

1 Because of population growth, the global demand for fish has more than doubled in the past three decades. Many fish populations are now dwindling as a direct result and North Sea Cod are thought to be on the verge of becoming endangered.

In Europe, fishing quotas have been reduced to try to control the number of fish caught, and some fishing fleets have even been decommissioned. Many fishermen are protesting against these actions, whilst conservationists think that not enough is being done.

a) In terms of sustainable development, why are fishing quotas important?

b) Over-fishing could lead to the extinction of some species. Describe one immediate effect this would have on…

i) the environment

ii) the human population.

c) Choose from the options provided below to fill in the gaps and complete this passage about the effects of quotas on fishing communities.

economy   tourism   limit   income   quotas   boats   decommissioning

The reduction of fishing _____, means that fishermen have to _____ their weekly catch. This affects their _____ and means that some cannot afford to maintain their _____ and are being driven out of business. This and the _____ of some fishing fleets, is having a dramatic effect on the local _____. Many fishing communities are now forced to rely on _____ as their main industry.

Unit 1 – Key Words

[Crossword grid]

Across

1. Resources that can be maintained (11)
7. A spontaneous change in the genetic material of a cell (8)
8. A nerve cell (7)
11. Changes to a species, which help it survive in a particular environment (10)
12. Describes the behaviour of an animal that preys on other animals (9)
14. A preparation containing a modified pathogen; used to produce immunity (7)
17. A chemical produced by the body and involved in homeostasis (7)
21. Metabolic… (4)
22. The permanent removal of large numbers of trees (13)
26. A hormone that helps control the cycle in 18 Down (2)
27. To no longer exist (7)
29. This type of disease occurs in people whose diets lack essential elements (10)
30. A pesticide will kill this (3)
31. An organism that is genetically identical to its parent (5)
32. An unborn animal (5)
33. The remains of an organism preserved in rock (6)
34. A chemical that speeds up reactions which take place in the cells (6)

Down

1. This type of fat is unhealthy (9)
2. The small gap between two neurones (7)
3. A cluster of cells, which develop into a 32 Across (6)
4. A cancer-causing chemical (10)
5. The variety of organisms and ecosystems in the natural world (12)
6. Receiving inadequate nourishment (12)
9. To change and develop over time (6)
10. Differences between individuals of the same species (9)
13. The substance that 15 Down and 28 Down are made of (3)
15. Found in the nuclei of cells, this carries genetic information (10)
16. This produces a response to a stimulus detected by a receptor (8)
18. The cycle by which a woman's body produces and releases eggs (9)
20. A superbug that is associated with poor hospital hygiene (4)
23. The hormone that stimulates oestrogen production (3)
24. A poison (5)
25. A mineral such as sodium (3)
28. A section of a chromosome (4)

Unit 2 – 12.1

Typical Plant and Animal Cells

1 Use the words below to label the two cell diagrams.

Plant Cell	Animal Cell	Cell Wall	Chloroplasts	Ribosomes
Cell Membrane	Cytoplasm	Nucleus	Vacuole	Chloroplasts

2 Write the correct word alongside each definition.

a) The wall of a plant cell is made from this. _____

b) Most cells have one of these; it contains genetic information. _____

c) Chloroplasts contain this light-absorbing substance. _____

d) All cells have one of these; it controls the movement of substances into and out of the cell. _____

3 Draw a line to connect each of the cells below to its correct description.

Nerve cells (neurones) have long slender structures which can carry nerve impulses over distances as long as one metre.

The sperm cell is the most mobile cell because of its tail. It has to travel from the vagina to the ovum.

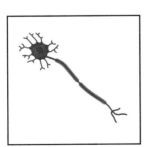

Red blood cells have no nucleus so that they can be packed full of haemoglobin in order to carry lots of oxygen.

White blood cells can change their shape in order to engulf and destroy microbes which have invaded the body.

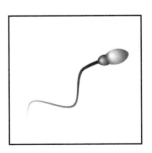

How Science Works

To answer the questions on this page, you will have to recall scientific facts and draw upon your knowledge of how science works, e.g. scientific procedures, issues and ideas.

1) When an organism is in the first stages of development, all of its cells are the same. They then differentiate and become specialised. What is the reason for specialisation?

....

2) The organelles (parts of a cell) found in muscle cells include…

- cell membrane
- nucleus
- lots of mitochondria
- fibres that slide into each other, so the cell can change length
- cytoplasm (called sarcoplasm)

a) Which of these organelles can be found in other animal cells?

....

b) Which of these organelles is unique to the muscle cell?

....

c) Think about the role of muscles in the body. Why do you think it is important for muscle cells…

i) to be able to change length?

....

....

ii) to contain lots of mitochondria?

....

....

3) Ciliated epithelial cells in the windpipe have tiny hair-like structures called cilia on the surface. When the cilia on lots of epithelial cells move together in a rhythmic motion, they can 'sweep' mucus away.

a) Ciliated epithelial cells always occur in large groups that form a tissue. Suggest one reason for this.

....

b) Suggest one other place where you would expect to find ciliated epithelial cells.

....

BIOLOGY WORKBOOK – Revision Guide Reference: Page 51

Unit 2 – 12.2

Diffusion

1 Why is it important for substances to be able to pass through the cell membrane to enter and leave a cell?

_____

_____

2 Insert an arrow between the two boxes below, to indicate the direction in which particles move during diffusion.

| Low Concentration | | High Concentration |

3 Write **true** or **false**, as appropriate, alongside each of these statements about diffusion.

a) Diffusion is a passive process – it takes place automatically, without the need for energy. _____

b) Diffusion can only take place through a cell membrane in one direction. _____

c) Oxygen, glucose and ions all enter the cell from the blood by diffusion. _____

d) Particles automatically move from a low concentration to a high concentration. _____

e) Diffusion takes place where there is a concentration gradient, i.e. the concentration of particles inside the cell is different to the concentration of particles outside the cell. _____

Osmosis

4 Insert an arrow between the two boxes below, to indicate the direction in which water molecules move during osmosis.

| Low Concentration | | High Concentration |

5 Sarah takes a beaker of water and adds some red food colouring. She then places a stalk of celery into the beaker and leaves it for 2 days. When Sarah returns, she finds that the leaves of the celery have turned red. Explain how this happened.

_____

_____

_____

Unit 2 – 12.3

Making Food Using Energy from the Sun

1 Write a dictionary-style definition for the word 'photosynthesis'. Remember, dictionary definitions use just a few well-chosen words to communicate an idea.

....

....

2 What four things are needed for photosynthesis?

a) .... b) ....

c) .... d) ....

3 Name each of the products of photosynthesis and, for each one, explain how the plant uses it.

a) ....

....

b) ....

....

4 Complete the equation below to show the reaction that takes place during photosynthesis.

.... + ... ⟶ .... + ...

5 What substance, found in green plants, absorbs the light needed for photosynthesis?

....

Factors Affecting Photosynthesis

6 The rate of photosynthesis in a plant slows down considerably in the evening. Suggest two possible reasons why this happens.

a) ....

b) ....

Unit 2 – 12.3

Factors Affecting Photosynthesis (cont.)

7 A plant is placed in a sealed glass box. A constant temperature and light intensity are maintained and the plant is watered regularly.

a) Sketch a graph to show what you would expect to happen to the rate of photosynthesis over time.

b) Explain what is happening in your graph.

Plant Mineral Requirements

8 Plants need certain mineral ions for healthy growth.

a) Where do these mineral ions come from? _____

b) How are these mineral ions taken in by the plant?

c) Why do plants need…

  i) nitrates? _____

  ii) magnesium? _____

9 Jenna is growing some bamboo shoots in a glass of water on her window sill. They receive plenty of sunlight and are kept at a constant temperature, however, the leaves start to turn yellow. Suggest one possible reason for this.

How Science Works

To answer the questions on this page, you will have to recall scientific facts and draw upon your knowledge of how science works, e.g. scientific procedures, issues and ideas.

1 A keen gardener is thinking about setting up a small business, selling home-grown strawberries. However, strawberries can be easily damaged by frost, so he decides to try growing some in a greenhouse.

He grows 100 plants in the greenhouse and 100 plants on the plot of land outside. The greenhouse uses natural light and air, but the temperature is kept at a constant 25°C.

Group (100 Strawberry Plants)	Fruit Yield (kg)
Plants Grown in Greenhouse	43kg
Plants Grown Outdoors	28kg

The table above right shows the fruit yield of the two groups of plants.

a) Write a short conclusion based on these results.

b) To ensure a fair test, it is important to control the variables. Suggest two other factors that could have affected the results of this investigation.

i) ....

ii) ....

c) The optimum yield of strawberry plants is 0.5kg per plant.

i) What would be the optimum yield of 100 plants? ....

ii) Suggest one possible reason why the greenhouse plants in this investigation did not achieve this optimum yield.

2 In terms of commercial fruit growing, name one other advantage of growing plants in a greenhouse.

3 In terms of pest control, suggest one advantage of growing plants in a greenhouse.

Unit 2 – 12.4

Food Chains

1 Complete the flow chart, using the words below, to show the order in which energy is transferred along a food chain.

| Primary Consumer | Tertiary Consumer | Secondary Consumer | Producer |

☐ → ☐ → ☐ → ☐

2 What is the original source of energy for all organisms? _____

3 Why are producers so important to a food chain?

4 Producers all belong to the same group. Indicate which group, by putting a tick beside the correct option.

a) Herbivores ☐   b) Insects ☐   c) Carnivores ☐   d) Green plants ☐   e) Omnivores ☐

5 Describe how energy is lost at each stage of a food chain.

Pyramids of Biomass

6 What is meant by the term 'biomass'?

7 Why does biomass decrease stage by stage as you move up a pyramid of biomass?

8 Describe how the efficiency of food production in a food chain can be improved.

How Science Works

To answer the questions on this page, you will have to recall scientific facts and draw upon your knowledge of how science works, e.g. scientific procedures, issues and ideas.

1 Sketch a pyramid of biomass for each of the food chains shown below.

a) **Hosta (green plant)** ⟶ **Slug** ⟶ **Hedgehog** ⟶ **Badger**

b) **Green Algae** ⟶ **Tadpoles** ⟶ **Raft Spider** ⟶ **Fish** ⟶ **Otter**

How Science Works

To answer the questions on this page, you will have to recall scientific facts and draw upon your knowledge of how science works, e.g. scientific procedures, issues and ideas.

1) A farmer breeds cattle for beef. The animals are kept in enclosures inside a barn so that the temperature can be regulated and they cannot move around too much.

a) In terms of food production, explain why the farmer would want to…

   i) regulate the temperature of the environment in which the cows are kept.

   ....

   ....

   ii) restrict how much the cattle can move around.

   ....

   ....

b) Suggest one other advantage of keeping the cows inside a barn like this.

....

c) Suggest one disadvantage for the farmer of raising cattle in this way.

....

d) Some people object to livestock being raised in this way. Suggest one reason for this.

....

e) There are strict guidelines and regulations in place to control the way in which farmers raise beef cattle. For example, it is prohibited to tie the animals up, because they need to be able to move freely and behave naturally.

Use the Internet (e.g. www.rspca.org.uk), school library or another secondary source to find one more example of a guideline relating to the care of beef cattle. Explain the reason for the guideline.

Guideline: ....

....

Reason: ....

....

Unit 2 – 12.5

Recycling the Materials of Life

1 Producers take materials from the environment to help them live and grow. These materials are eventually returned to the environment. Name the two ways in which this happens.

a) ....

b) ....

2 a) In your own words, explain the role of microorganisms in this process.

....

....

b) Humans have learnt to use these microorganisms to help get rid of waste materials. Outline one example of this in practice.

....

....

The Carbon Cycle

3 Write the appropriate number alongside each explanation below, to show what stage of the carbon cycle it is describing.

a) Animals release CO_2 (a product of respiration) into the air. ☐

b) Microorganisms break down excrement and the bodies of dead animals and plants. ☐

c) Green plants take CO_2 from the atmosphere for photosynthesis. Some is returned during respiration. ☐

d) Microorganisms release CO_2 (a product of respiration) into the air. ☐

e) Carbon is converted into carbohydrates, fats and proteins by plants. When the plant is eaten, some of this carbon is then converted into carbohydrates, fats and proteins in the animal. ☐

Unit 2 – 12.6

Enzymes

1 a) Unscramble the letters to find three words that can be used to describe enzymes.

   i) SCATTLAYS ....

   ii) TENIPOR ....

   iii) ADOMINICAS ....

b) Write a brief description of what an enzyme is, incorporating your three answers from part **a)**.

....

....

....

2 What is special about the shape of enzymes?

....

3 What two factors can affect the action of enzymes?

   a) ....   b) ....

4 a) What is the normal body temperature of a human being? ....

b) In terms of enzymes, explain why it is important for humans to maintain a fairly constant body temperature.

....

....

Inside Living Cells

5 Name two processes that occur in living cells and involve enzymes.

   a) ....

   b) ....

6 Respiration in cells is the process by which glucose molecules are broken down to release energy. Describe one way in which this energy is used.

....

Unit 2 – 12.6

Aerobic Respiration

1 a) The parts of the body that enable breathing, e.g. the windpipe, lungs and diaphragm, are often referred to as the respiratory system. What is the difference between breathing and respiration?

b) Which gas must be present for aerobic respiration to be able to take place?

c) Write a word equation for aerobic respiration.

d) In what part of a living cell does aerobic respiration usually take place?

Outside Living Cells

2 What is the function of digestive enzymes?

3 Complete the table below to show where the different digestive enzymes can be found, what substances they digest and what molecules are produced.

Enzyme	Regions Where It is Found	What It Digests	Molecules Produced
Protease	• • •		Amino Acids
	• Pancreas • Small Intestine	Lipids	
Amylase	• • •	Starch	

4 What are lipids?

Unit 2 – 12.6

The Function of Bile

1 Where is bile…

a) produced? _____ b) stored? _____

c) Summarise the two main functions of bile.

   i) _____

   ii) _____

2 Many people suffer from gallstones. This can result in the removal of the gall bladder. State two possible problems this could cause.

a) _____

b) _____

Use of Enzymes in the Home and Industry

3 Washing detergents for clothes are described as biological or non-biological. Biological detergents contain enzymes. How does this help them to clean clothes more effectively?

_____

_____

4 Explain how enzymes are used in the production of baby foods.

_____

_____

5 a) What function does isomerase perform?

_____

b) How do manufacturers take advantage of this in the production of slimming foods?

_____

How Science Works

To answer the questions on this page, you will have to recall scientific facts and draw upon your knowledge of how science works, e.g. scientific procedures, issues and ideas.

1 What is the function of enzymes?

_____

2 a) How can enzymes help manufacturers save energy?

_____

b) How does this benefit the environment?

_____

3 Describe two ways in which enzymes can be used in industry (other than those outlined on page 61).

a) _____

_____

b) _____

_____

4 The manufacturers of biological washing powders recommend that you only use the powder for cool washes (up to 40°C).

a) Why is this?

_____

b) Give one disadvantage of using enzymes in washing powders.

_____

5 Choose the correct words from the options below to complete this passage about one of the problems associated with using enzymes in industry.

| **re-use** | **liquids** | **immobilised** | **non-reactive** | **expensive** | **soluble** |

Extracting enzymes is _____, so it is important to be able to _____ them as often as possible. However, enzymes are _____ in water, which makes it difficult to remove them from _____ after use if they are not _____ first, i.e. trapped inside a _____ material.

Unit 2 – 12.7

Controlling Conditions

1 a) Which organ is responsible for monitoring and controlling blood glucose concentration? ....

b) Which hormone does it produce to help maintain blood glucose levels? ....

c) How does this hormone work?

....

....

Blood Glucose Concentration

2 Use the descriptions provided to complete the flow chart and show what happens when blood glucose concentration is too high.

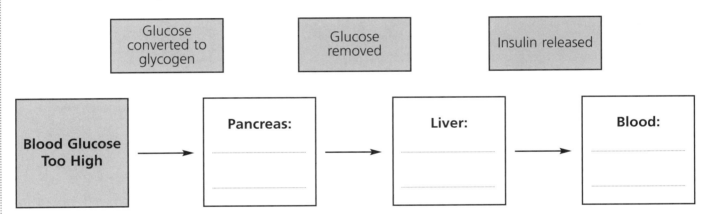

3 a) What causes diabetes?

....

....

b) Name two ways in which blood glucose concentrations can be controlled in people with diabetes.

  i) ....

  ii) ....

Unit 2 – 12.7

Body Temperature

1 Body temperature is controlled by the nervous system.

   a) Where are the receptors that provide information about blood temperature located? _____

   b) Where are the receptors that provide information about skin temperature located? _____

2 Explain why is it important to drink more water in hot weather.

_____

_____

HT

3 Write **hot** or **cold** alongside each of these responses, to show the temperature conditions that trigger them.

   a) Any sweating stops. _____

   b) Blood vessels close to the skin's surface dilate. _____

   c) Blood vessels close to the skin's surface constrict. _____

4 In terms of heat loss, explain how the dilation or contraction of blood vessels close to the skin's surface helps to regulate temperature.

_____

_____

Removing Waste Products

5 Name two waste products that need to be removed from the body to maintain a constant internal environment. For each answer, state which process it is a product of and how it is removed.

   a) Waste Product: _____

   A product of… _____

   Removed by… _____

   b) Waste Product: _____

   A product of… _____

   Removed by… _____

How Science Works

To answer the questions on this page, you will have to recall scientific facts and draw upon your knowledge of how science works, e.g. scientific procedures, issues and ideas.

1 In the early 20th century, experiments carried out by Banting and Best led to the development of an effective treatment for diabetes.

a) How did Banting and Best establish that diabetes is linked to a problem with the pancreas?

b) In their subsequent experiments, what did the two scientists inject into diabetic dogs to try to control the disease?

c) To produce a fair test, it is important to control the variables. Which variable did Banting and Best struggle to control?

d) Banting and Best repeated their experiments many times with the same results. Why is it important to be able to do this?

e) Banting and Best carried out their research on dogs. In terms of understanding human diabetes, why might this have been a problem?

f) Which hormone was discovered as a result of Banting and Best's experiments?

g) Before announcing their findings, Banting and Best only treated one human. Suggest a potential problem with this…

   i) in terms of producing reliable evidence.

   ii) in terms of modern procedures for developing new drugs.

How Science Works

To answer the questions on this page, you will have to recall scientific facts and draw upon your knowledge of how science works, e.g. scientific procedures, issues and ideas.

1 Insulin is used to help manage blood sugar levels in people with diabetes. It can be administered by injection or through an inhaler.

  a) Which method has been around the longest? _____

  b) Is it an **advantage** or a **disadvantage** that this method has been around for a long time? Explain your answer.

  _____
  _____
  _____

2 Describe two factors that can affect the absorption of injected insulin into the bloodstream.

  a) _____

  b) _____

3 Why are insulin injections sometimes less effective in patients that smoke?

  _____
  _____

4 Suggest two benefits of inhaling insulin.

  a) _____

  b) _____

5 Why might insulin inhalers be more expensive than injections?

  _____

6 Name one other potential problem with insulin inhalers.

  _____

7 If insulin inhalers prove to be safe and effective, suggest one age group that might really benefit.

  _____

Unit 2 – 12.8

Chromosomes

1 For each question, indicate the correct answer by placing a tick in the box alongside it.

a) Human body cells contain a total of…

i) 23 chromosomes ☐

ii) 46 chromosomes ☐

iii) 22 chromosomes ☐

b) Sex cells are called…

i) genes ☐

ii) alleles ☐

iii) gametes ☐

c) Sex cells contain…

i) half the number of chromosomes of a body cell ☐

ii) the same number of chromosomes as a body cell ☐

iii) twice the number of chromosomes of a body cell ☐

Inheritance of Sex – The Sex Chromosome

2 Below are two sets of sex chromosomes. Write **male** or **female** alongside each one, to identify the sex of the individual they come from.

a) XY _____   b) XX _____

3 Complete the genetic diagram below, to show all the possible permutations for sex inheritance.

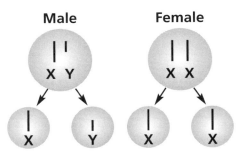

Unit 2 – 12.8

Cell Division

1 The following flow chart shows **mitosis**. Complete the chart by drawing a diagram for each stage.

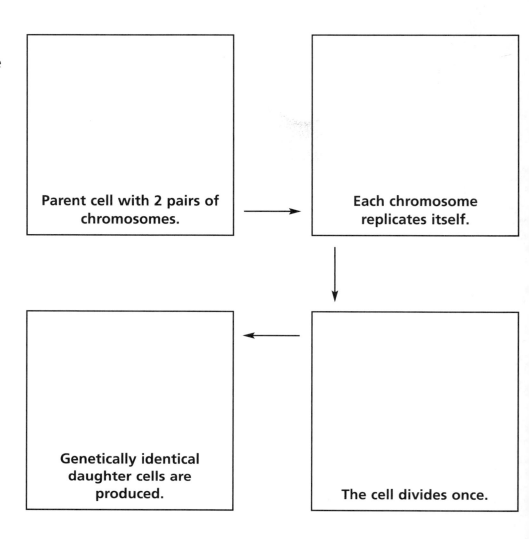

2 Use a line to connect the words 'meiosis' and 'mitosis' to the correct statements.

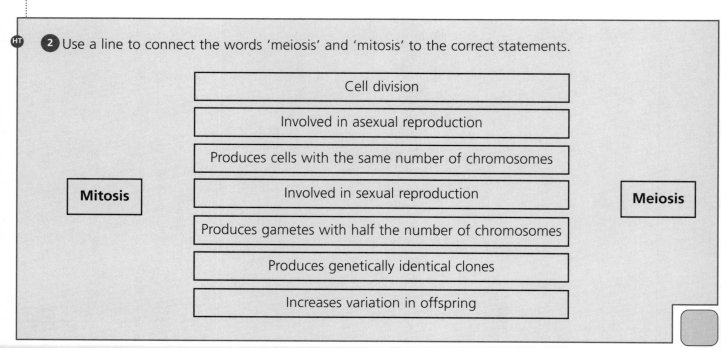

Unit 2 – 12.8

Genetics

1 Write dictionary-style definitions for the following words. Remember, dictionary definitions only use a few well-chosen words.

a) Allele _____

b) Dominant Allele _____

c) Recessive Allele _____

2 a) T is the allele for having the ability to roll the tongue and t is the allele for not being able to roll the tongue. State whether the following individuals can roll their tongues or not.

i) tt _____ ii) TT _____

iii) tT _____ iv) Tt _____

b) B is the allele for brown eyes and b is the allele for blue eyes. State the colour of the following individuals' eyes.

i) Bb _____ ii) bB _____

iii) bb _____ iv) BB _____

3 Scientists discovered a new species of plant, which occurs naturally in two different sizes. The height of the plant is determined by a single gene, which has two alleles. H is the dominant allele for tall plants, h is the allele for short plants.

List all the possible combination of alleles for this gene. For each combination, state whether the plant would be **tall** or **short** and whether it is **homozygous dominant, heterozygous** or **homozygous recessive.**

a) _____

b) _____

c) _____

4 State whether the following combinations of genes are **homozygous dominant, heterozygous** or **homozygous recessive**.

a) Tt _____ b) BB _____

c) ee _____ d) Bb _____

Unit 2 – 12.8

Monohybrid Inheritance and Inheritance of Eye-Colour

1 a) Complete these two different crosses between a brown-eyed parent and a blue-eyed parent.

i) Brown Eyes x Blue Eyes

Parents: BB × bb

Gametes: B, B, b, b

ii) Brown Eyes x Blue Eyes

Parents: Bb × bb

Gametes: B, b, b, b

Offspring:

Colour: _____

b) For each of the crosses in part **a)**, what is the percentage chance of a child having blue eyes?

i) _____ ii) _____

2 Explain how two parents with brown eyes could produce children with blue eyes. Use a diagram to help.

_____
_____
_____
_____

3 Put a tick alongside the definition that best describes monohybrid inheritance.

a) Monohybrid inheritance occurs when a characteristic is controlled by several genes working together. ☐

b) Monohybrid inheritance occurs when a characteristic is controlled by multiple alleles. ☐

c) Monohybrid inheritance occurs when a characteristic is determined by a single gene, i.e. one pair of alleles. ☐

Unit 2 – 12.8

Differentiation of Cells

1 Use the words provided to complete this passage about differentiation.

| differentiation | features | specialised | organism | structure | functions |

All of the cells in a living _____ start out the same. They then become _____. That is to say, they develop a _____ with special _____, which helps them to perform specific _____. This process is called _____.

2 Stem cells are cells that have not yet differentiated.

a) Why does this make them ideal for certain medical applications?

_____

b) Name two places where human stem cells can be found.

i) _____   ii) _____

HT

3 Use the words provided to complete this passage about genes.

| sequence | organism | instructions | cell | DNA | amino acids |

A gene is a section of _____, which acts as a code. This code provides _____ for making a particular protein by determining the _____ used and the _____ in which they are joined. The resulting proteins control how the individual _____ functions and how the _____ as a whole develops.

4 Draw a diagram to show all the possible outcomes of a cross between a mother who is heterozygous for Huntington's disease (Hh) and a father who is healthy (hh).

How Science Works

To answer the questions on this page, you will have to recall scientific facts and draw upon your knowledge of how science works, e.g. scientific procedures, issues and ideas.

1) In the late 19th century, Gregor Mendel observed that in pea plants there were just two possible outcomes for height: tall or dwarf.

His experiments led him to identify 'determiners', which we now know to be genes.

In his initial experiments Mendel crossed a pure-breeding tall plant with a pure-breeding dwarf plant, producing offspring that were all tall.

a) If the height of pea plants is determined by a single gene…

   i) which characteristic is dominant? _____

   ii) which characteristic is recessive? _____

b) Draw a genetic diagram to illustrate this cross. Use T for the dominant characteristic and t for the recessive one.

c) In his second stage of experiments, Mendel crossed two of the offspring from his initial experiments. In the resulting offspring, there was one dwarf plant for every three tall plants. Draw a genetic diagram to illustrate this cross.

d) Mendel used over 21 000 plants in his experiments. Explain why it was important for him to perform the same experiments using lots of different plants.

_____

_____

_____

How Science Works

To answer the questions on this page, you will have to recall scientific facts and draw upon your knowledge of how science works, e.g. scientific procedures, issues and ideas.

1 a) Why do some people believe that embryos should be treated like people?

....

....

b) Why do others disagree?

....

....

c) Which of the above groups do you think is most likely to disagree with stem cells being extracted from embryos for medical purposes?

....

2 For people with certain diseases, stem cell therapy could provide relief from symptoms and extend their life expectancy.

a) In terms of the patient's quality of life, what effect do you think this will have?

....

b) In terms of population size, what effect do you think this will have?

....

c) Suggest two ways in which this might impact on society. (Hint: think about things like housing and employment.)

i) ....

ii) ....

3 a) Most of the embryos used in stem cell research are left over from IVF treatments. How are these embryos produced?

....

....

b) With reference to Question 1, why do you think it is important to get the couple's consent before using their embryos for stem cell research?

....

....

How Science Works

To answer the questions on this page, you will have to recall scientific facts and draw upon your knowledge of how science works, e.g. scientific procedures, issues and ideas.

1 If it became common practice to screen embryos for 'faulty' genes and abort those with defects, certain diseases and disorders could eventually be completely eliminated.

   a) Below are some of the arguments for and against this practice. Write **for** or **against** alongside each one.

   i) The money that is currently spent treating these diseases could be put to use elsewhere. ....

   ii) Disease is a natural way of controlling the population. ....

   iii) It would devalue the lives of people currently living with disease. ....

   iv) It would prevent unnecessary pain and suffering. ....

   v) An embryo is a new life; destroying it is murder. ....

   vi) It would free up hospital beds and resources for other patients. ....

   b) Select one argument from part **a)** that is concerned with economics (i.e. money).

   ....

   c) Select one argument from part **a)** that is concerned with society (i.e. the overall impact on the population).

   ....

   d) Select one argument from part **a)** that is concerned with ethics (i.e. what is morally accepted).

   ....

2 There are concerns that people might start using genetic screening methods to select the sex and characteristics of their children.

   a) Give one ethical argument against this.

   ....

   b) In terms of variation, explain how this could affect the population.

   ....

   ....

How Science Works

To answer the questions on this page, you will have to recall scientific facts and draw upon your knowledge of how science works, e.g. scientific procedures, issues and ideas.

1 Cystic fibrosis is an inherited disorder, caused by a recessive allele.

a) Draw a diagram to show all the possible outcomes of a cross between a mother who has cystic fibrosis (cc) and a father who does not (CC).

b) What is the percentage chance that their offspring will be heterozygous for the disorder?

c) With the aid of a diagram, explain how a couple, neither of whom have cystic fibrosis, could have a child with cystic fibrosis.

Unit 2 – Key Words

1 Alongside each of the following definitions, write the word being described.

a) A catalyst that increases the rate of biochemical reactions (6)
b) A collection of similar cells which work together to perform a function (6)
c) A collection of tissues which work together to perform a particular function (5)
d) A fluid-filled sac found inside plant cells (7)
e) A fundamental unit of a living organism (4)
f) A specialised sex cell (6)
g) A substance that increases the rate of a chemical reaction (8)
h) Will not dissolve; a property (9)
i) A toxin produced when proteins are broken down (4)
j) Allows substances to pass through (9)
k) An alternative form of a gene (6)
l) An enzyme that breaks down fat into fatty acids and glycerol (6)
m) An enzyme that breaks down starch (7)
n) An enzyme used to break down proteins (8)
o) Developed for a specific function (11)
p) Natural decomposition (5)
q) Respiration in the absence of oxygen (9)
r) Respiration using oxygen (7)
s) The ability to dissolve (7)
t) The automatic movement of particles along a concentration gradient (9)
u) The automatic movement of water along a concentration gradient (7)
v) The division of a cell to form two daughter cells with the same number of chromosomes as the parent (7)
w) The division of a parent cell to form two daughter cells with half its number of chromosomes (7)
x) The fusion of a male gamete with a female gamete (13)
y) The greenish-yellow liquid produced by the liver (4)
z) The main operating temperature of an organism (4)
aa) The maintenance of a constant body temperature (16)
bb) The mass of living material in an organism (7)
cc) The measure of acidity (2)
dd) The narrowest type of blood vessel (9)
ee) The part of a cell involved in protein synthesis (9)
ff) The part of a plant cell that contains chlorophyll (11)
gg) The pigment found in green plants that is responsible for photosynthesis (11)
hh) The process by which plants produce glucose using light energy (14)
ii) The soft tissue found inside bones (6)
jj) The substance from which chromosomes are made (3)
kk) The substance outside the nucleus of a cell, in which the organelles are suspended (9)
ll) The waste product produced by the kidneys (5)
mm) Very small organisms, often single cells (13)

Unit 2 – Key Words

2 Find all your answers to Question 1 in the wordsearch below.

T	H	E	R	M	O	R	E	G	U	L	A	T	I	O	N	T	G	O	D	S
I	I	M	I	C	R	O	O	R	G	A	N	I	S	M	S	A	A	N	I	P
A	E	R	O	B	I	C	S	S	L	S	U	N	N	Y	M	S	N	E		
M	D	A	Y	A	N	D	W	H	S	E	L	S	N	I	F	I	E	N	S	C
Y	I	S	C	A	P	I	L	L	A	R	Y	U	H	W	O	H	T	E	O	I
L	R	M	C	K	I	A	M	G	M	P	H	E	O	E	T	I	E	L	L	A
A	N	A	E	R	O	B	I	C	O	N	P	G	T	N	O	B	U	B	U	L
S	Y	R	L	A	N	I	I	C	I	E	O	O	Y	Z	C	E	R	U	B	I
E	E	R	L	L	A	L	M	A	B	N	R	S	D	Y	S	L	I	L	L	S
R	T	O	O	U	E	E	T	S	I	G	O	D	E	M	I	B	N	O	E	E
O	T	W	D	H	E	L	S	U	A	T	L	N	G	E	O	A	M	S	O	D
C	D	L	N	U	C	K	E	N	O	W	H	I	V	T	H	E	E	Y	O	I
C	A	T	A	L	Y	S	T	H	U	E	C	R	A	E	X	M	I	A	M	F
O	C	H	L	O	R	O	P	L	A	S	T	S	C	I	O	R	O	H	O	U
P	S	E	Y	U	R	I	N	E	O	A	E	R	U	S	U	E	S	F	I	S
N	D	M	T	D	E	C	A	Y	H	E	I	S	O	B	O	P	I	O	K	S
C	Y	T	O	P	L	A	S	M	U	T	S	B	L	I	P	A	S	E	E	I
M	I	T	O	S	I	S	F	U	L	O	I	W	E	E	W	A	N	T	Y	O
O	U	T	O	D	I	O	W	F	E	R	T	I	L	I	S	A	T	I	O	N
N	U	C	L	E	U	S	E	L	L	P	V	X	Y	B	C	D	N	T	O	L

BIOLOGY WORKBOOK – Revision Guide Reference: Page 79

Unit 3 – 13.1

Active Transport

1 Choose the correct option to complete each of the following sentences. Put a line through the two wrong answers.

a) Active transport…

   i) does not require energy

   ii) requires energy from respiration

   iii) requires electrical energy

b) During active transport, substances move…

   i) against the concentration gradient

   ii) along the concentration gradient

   iii) in random directions

c) Diffusion and osmosis…

   i) are examples of active transport

   ii) are not examples of active transport

   iii) do not involve the movement of substances

Exchanging Material in Humans

2 a) Name two organ systems within the human body that are specialised to aid the exchange of materials.

   i) _____ ii) _____

b) Name two properties that the organ systems above have in common, and explain how each one helps to create an efficient exchange surface.

   i) _____

   ii) _____

3 a) Describe the exchange process that takes place in the lungs.

b) Is this process an example of active transport? Explain your answer.

Unit 3 – 13.1

Exchange in Plants

1 By what process do plants lose water vapour from their leaves?

....

....

2 A student conducted an experiment to see what would happen to a young plant when it was deprived of water. The plant was placed in a pot and left in a warm room without being watered. After a few days the plant had wilted. Explain in detail…

a) how plants lose water.

....

....

b) why the plant wilted after a few days.

....

....

3 a) Explain what a plant can do to reduce water loss.

....

b) As a result of the plant reducing water loss in this way, what other process will be slowed down?

....

c) Explain why this process is slowed down when water loss is reduced.

....

....

d) Which cells are responsible for controlling the size of the stomata?

....

4 Broad-leaved plants lose their leaves in winter. Apply your knowledge of water loss and wilting to explain why this is a good survival strategy.

....

....

How Science Works

To answer the questions on this page, you will have to recall scientific facts and draw upon your knowledge of how science works, e.g. scientific procedures, issues and ideas.

1 What two features help an exchange surface to function efficiently?

a) ....

b) ....

2 Choose one of the following three examples of exchange surfaces. Explain how the exchange surface is adapted to maximise effectiveness and draw a diagram to support your explanation. Remember to state which substances are exchanged at the surface.

a) The outer surface of a flatworm.

b) The gills of a fish.

c) The lungs of a human or mammal.

Unit 3 – 13.2

The Circulation System

1 The diagram alongside shows the circulation system.

a) What is the function of the circulation system?

....

....

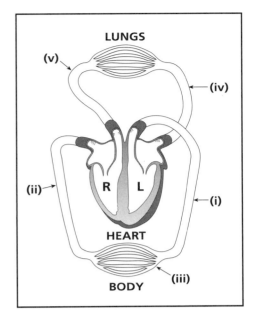

b) Name the type of blood vessels labelled.

   i) ....   ii) ....

   iii) ....   iv) ....

   v) ....

c) On the diagram, colour deoxygenated blood blue and oxygenated blood red.

d) On the diagram, clearly label with arrows, the direction of blood flow around the circulation system.

e) Why is this system called a 'double circulation system'?

....

The Blood

2 Blood carries oxygen around the body. Which part of the blood carries the oxygen?

....

3 The amount of oxygen in the atmosphere decreases as you climb in altitude.

a) Why do people who live at high altitude have more red blood cells?

....

b) Athletes often train at high altitude before a big race. How does this help their performance?

....

4 Describe three specific functions of blood plasma.

   a) ....

   b) ....

   c) ....

Unit 3 – 13.3

Aerobic Respiration

1) What is the difference between breathing and respiration?

....

....

2) a) What gas has to be present for aerobic respiration to take place?

....

b) Which other substance is needed for respiration?

....

c) What is the main purpose of aerobic respiration?

....

d) Which waste products are produced during respiration?

....

e) Write a word equation for aerobic respiration.

....

Anaerobic Respiration

3) A girl is playing football. She sprints the length of the field to score the winning goal. However, she can barely celebrate because her legs have gone weak and rubbery and she cannot get her breath back.

a) What type of respiration produces these effects?

....

HT

b) Write a word equation for this type of respiration.

....

c) Explain, in as much detail as you can, why the girl's legs felt weak and rubbery.

....

....

Unit 3 – 13.3

Aerobic and Anaerobic Respiration

4 a) In terms of the amount of energy released, how much more efficient is aerobic respiration compared to anaerobic respiration? Indicate the correct answer with a tick.

   i) 5 times more efficient ☐

   ii) 10 times more efficient ☐

   iii) 20 times more efficient ☐

   iv) 40 times more efficient ☐

b) Why is aerobic respiration more efficient than anaerobic respiration?

....

....

c) Give one advantage of anaerobic respiration.

....

5 The coach of a football team makes the players take part in interval training. This involves jogging for 30 seconds, sprinting for 15 seconds, jogging for 30 seconds, sprinting for 15 seconds and so on.

a) Explain why the players are not out of breath after the first 30 second jog.

....

....

b) Explain why they are out of breath every time they return to a jog after sprinting.

....

....

6 Explain what is meant by the term 'oxygen debt' and describe how it must be repaid.

....

....

How Science Works

To answer the questions on this page, you will have to recall scientific facts and draw upon your knowledge of how science works, e.g. scientific procedures, issues and ideas.

1) A man is running in a long distance race.
A graph of his heart rate is shown alongside.

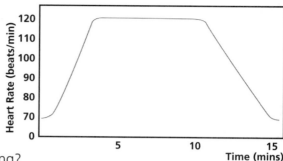

a) What happens to the man's heart rate when he starts running?

b) What will happen to the man's breathing?

c) Use your knowledge of aerobic respiration to explain your answers to parts **a)** and **b)**.

2) A woman was competing in a long-distance race. During the race her blood-sugar level dropped.

a) Explain briefly, why blood-sugar levels are likely to drop during prolonged exercise.

b) Use your knowledge of aerobic respiration to explain how a drop in blood sugar level could stop the athlete from performing at her most efficient level.

c) Many athletes eat meals that are high in carbohydrates prior to a big race and take on extra glucose (in sports drinks, etc.) during the race. Why do you think they do this?

Unit 3 – 13.4

The Function of the Kidney

1 The kidney helps to maintain the internal environment of the body.

a) Name two important tissues in the kidney.

   i) .... ii) ....

b) What is the name of the tube which takes urine from the kidney?

c) What is the name of the organ where the urine is stored?

d) How much glucose would you normally expect to find in urine?

e) i) Name the substances that pass out of the blood into the tubules.

   ii) What name is given to this process?

f) Some substances that the body cannot afford to lose are reabsorbed into the blood.

   i) What is the name given to this process?

   ii) Glucose and ions have to be reabsorbed against a concentration gradient. What is this process called?

   iii) Where does the energy come from to enable the glucose and ions to be reabsorbed?

2 A cyclist goes for a long bike ride on a very hot day. Afterwards, she notices that her urine is very yellow. Why is her urine more yellow than normal and could this have been prevented? Explain your answer.

Unit 3 – 13.4

Using a Dialysis Machine

1 In what situation is it necessary to use a dialysis machine?

....

2 a) Explain, in as much detail as you can, how a dialysis machine simulates the functions of a kidney.

....

....

....

....

b) Why is it important for dialysis fluid to contain the same concentration of useful substances as the patient's blood?

....

Kidney Transplants

3 What is the purpose of a kidney transplant?

....

4 a) Explain why is it important for the tissue type of the donor kidney to closely match that of the recipient.

....

b) How is this best achieved?

....

c) Describe three other measures that can be taken to ensure the transplant is given every chance of success, and explain why they are important.

i) ....

....

ii) ....

....

iii) ....

....

How Science Works

To answer the questions on this page, you will have to recall scientific facts and draw upon your knowledge of how science works, e.g. scientific procedures, issues and ideas.

1 a) Name two causes of kidney failure.

   i) _____ ii) _____

b) Give three symptoms of kidney failure.

   i) _____

   ii) _____

   iii) _____

2 a) Name two advantages of dialysis, in comparison to kidney transplants.

   i) _____

   ii) _____

b) Name two disadvantages of dialysis.

   i) _____

   ii) _____

3 a) Name three advantages of a kidney transplant, in comparison to dialysis.

   i) _____

   ii) _____

   iii) _____

b) Name three disadvantages of a kidney transplant.

   i) _____

   ii) _____

   iii) _____

4 Is it possible for a living person to donate a kidney for transplant? Explain your answer.

_____

Unit 3 – 13.5

Yeast

1 What is yeast? Draw a diagram to illustrate your answer.

How Yeast Works

2 a) Write a word equation to show the reaction that takes place when yeast respires **anaerobically** in the presence of glucose.

b) What is the name given to this process?

3 Write a word equation to show the reaction that takes place when yeast respires **aerobically** in the presence of glucose.

4 Explain how yeast is responsible for making bread rise.

5 Explain how yeast is used to produce beer from barley.

How Science Works

To answer the questions on this page, you will have to recall scientific facts and draw upon your knowledge of how science works, e.g. scientific procedures, issues and ideas.

1 Aristotle's theory of abiogenesis, now known as spontaneous generation, stated that living organisms could be produced from non-living material through the process of decay. For example, he believed that when maggots appeared on rancid meat, it was because they have been produced from the meat spontaneously.

In 1768, Lazzaro Spallanzani put forward a theory that microorganisms could be found in the air.

a) Describe briefly the experiment that led him to this conclusion.

b) How did the results of Spallanzani's experiment contradict Aristotle's theory of abiogenesis?

2 In 1839, Theodore Schwann put forward the idea that would form the basis of a new theory called biogenesis.

What is the principle idea behind the theory of biogenesis?

3 a) Describe briefly the famous experiment carried out by Louis Pasteur.

b) How did Pasteur's findings support those of Spallanzani and Schwann?

Unit 3 – 13.6

Growing Microorganisms

1 Fill in the missing words to complete this passage about how microorganisms can be grown to produce useful products.

Microorganisms can be grown in large vessels called _____. These usually have an air supply, to provide _____ so that the microorganisms can respire, a _____ to keep the microorganisms in suspension and maintain an even _____, a water-cooled jacket to remove _____ produced by the respiring microorganisms, and instruments (e.g. probes) to monitor factors such as _____ and _____.

2 a) Which useful product can be made by growing the mould called penicillium?

b) What does the medium need to contain to grow penicillium?

3 a) Which useful product can be made by growing the fungus called Fusarium?

b) What does the medium need to contain to grow Fusarium?

4 a) What type of respiration is required for the fermentation of biofuels?

b) How can this be achieved?

5 a) Which materials can be used to produce ethanol-based fuels?

b) Name one practical use of ethanol-based fuels.

How Science Works

To answer the questions on this page, you will have to recall scientific facts and draw upon your knowledge of how science works, e.g. scientific procedures, issues and ideas.

1 Most of the fuels currently used in industry, in our homes and for transport are fossil fuels.

a) In terms of sustainable development why is this a problem?

....

b) In terms of the environment, why is this a problem?

....

2 a) List three advantages of using biogas compared to fossil fuels.

i) ....

ii) ....

iii) ....

b) Alongside each of your answers to part **a)**, write **Environment** or **Economy** to show whether the advantage benefits the environment or the economy.

c) List three disadvantages of using biogas compared to fossil fuels.

i) ....

ii) ....

iii) ....

d) Alongside each of your answers to part **c)**, write **Environment** or **Economy** to show whether the disadvantage affects the environment or the economy.

3 In Sweden, biogas is being produced from the parts of animals that cannot be sold as meat, to run public trains.

Use the Internet, library or another source to find one other example of how a European country is using biogas. Include details of the waste products being used in production, and how the biogas is being used.

....

....

....

....

How Science Works

To answer the questions on this page, you will have to recall scientific facts and draw upon your knowledge of how science works, e.g. scientific procedures, issues and ideas.

1 The diagrams below show two different types of biogas generator.

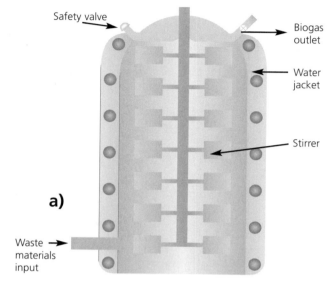

a)

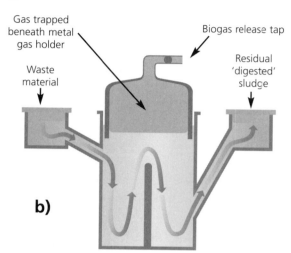

b)

a) What type of generator is shown in diagram **a)**?
....

b) What type of generator is shown in diagram **b)**?
....

c) Name two disadvantages to the type of generator shown in diagram **a)**.

   i) ....

   ii) ....

d) Name two disadvantages to the type of generator shown in diagram **b)**.

   i) ....

   ii) ....

e) Which generator is most likely to be used for the commercial production of biogas (i.e. on a large scale, for profit)? Explain your answer.
....
....
....
....

BIOLOGY WORKBOOK – Revision Guide Reference: Page 98

Unit 3 – 13.7

Preparing a Culture Medium

1 a) Name one substance commonly used as the base for a medium for growing microorganisms.

b) Unscramble the letters below to find four things that might be added to that base to provide ideal growing conditions for cultures.

i) SPINEROT

ii) LIARMEN ISON

iii) DRYSORTABEACH

iv) NATIVISM

2 a) What is an autoclave?

b) What is an inoculating loop?

c) Using the words 'autoclave' and 'inoculating loop', briefly describe the three steps that should be followed to ensure that a culture is not contaminated.

i) Step 1:

ii) Step 2:

iii) Step 3:

d) Why is it important that cultures do not become contaminated?

3 At school, why should cultures only be incubated at temperatures of 25°C or below?

Unit 3 – Key Words

1 Complete the crossword below.

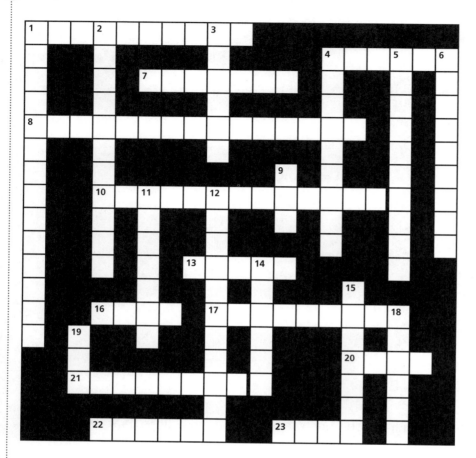

Across

1. The deficiency of a particular gas as a result of intense exercise (6, 4)
4. The clear fluid part of blood (6)
7. The movement of water along a concentration gradient (7)
8. The movement of substances against a concentration gradient (6, 9)
10. Plants lose water from their leaves by this process (13)
13. Projections on the wall of the small intestine (5)
16. To droop as a result of excess water loss (4)
17. Developed under controlled conditions in a laboratory (9)
20. To convert the starch in germinated barley to glucose (4)
21. The artificial removal of urea and excess material from the blood (8)
22. The name given to the substance in which a culture is grown (6)
23. A waste product formed in the kidneys (4)

Down

1. The combination of oxygen and the red pigment in blood (14)
2. The process by which a seed first begins to grow (11)
3. A fuel produced from the anaerobic fermentation of organic waste (6)
4. A round shallow container used to grow cultures (5, 4)
5. Free from all microorganisms (10)
6. The type of respiration that takes place in the absence of oxygen (9)
9. Methane occurs in this state (3)
11. Air sacs in the lungs (7)
12. The mould from which a certain type of antibiotic can be developed (11)
14. The type of acid produced during anaerobic respiration (6)
15. Pores in the under-surface of plant leaves (7)
18. To widen or enlarge (6)
19. The colour of the pigment, haemoglobin (3)

Unit 3 – Key Words

1 For each of the following words, place a tick beside the correct definition.

a) Aerobic
- **i)** In the presence of air. ☐
- **ii)** In the presence of carbon dioxide. ☐
- **iii)** In the presence of oxygen. ☐

b) Diffusion
- **i)** The movement of substances against a concentration gradient. ☐
- **ii)** The movement of substances along a concentration gradient. ☐
- **iii)** The movement of substances by artificial means. ☐

c) Fermentation
- **i)** The process by which sugar is converted into alcohol. ☐
- **ii)** The process by which glucose is converted into energy. ☐
- **iii)** The process by which glucose is produced by plants. ☐

d) Guard Cells
- **i)** The specialised cells found on the wall of the small intestine. ☐
- **ii)** The specialised cells found in plants, which absorb water from the soil. ☐
- **iii)** The specialised cells that open and close the stomata on leaves. ☐

e) Irradiation
- **i)** Exposure to radiation to kill microorganisms. ☐
- **ii)** The reversal of the effects of radiation. ☐
- **iii)** A method of supplying plants with water. ☐

f) Mycoprotein
- **i)** A very small protein molecule. ☐
- **ii)** A protein-rich food produced from fungi. ☐
- **iii)** An ingredient used in face creams. ☐

g) Methane
- **i)** An extremely light gas used in party balloons. ☐
- **ii)** A toxic gas produced during combustion. ☐
- **iii)** A clear gas given off by animal waste. ☐

Notes